MDO

MINDSET DETERMINES OUTCOME

An Inspirational Novel Based on True Events

DR. ZAAHIR HENDRICKS

MDO

MINDSET DETERMINES OUTCOME

An Inspirational Novel Based on True Events

DR. ZAAHIR HENDRICKS

MDO
MINDSET DETERMINES OUTCOME:
An Inspirational Novel Based on True Events
Copyright © 2012 by Dr. Zaahir Hendricks

ISBN: 978-0-9884697-0-9

Published in the United States of America by
www.mindsetdeterminesoutcome.com
A Division of Superb-Living

Cover design by Phil Scharer
Cover photo and editing by Dr. Ramzie

First paperback edition, 2012
Second paperback edition 2016

This book is dedicated to my family, my friends and my mentors for starting me on this journey of self-discovery so long ago.

To the family members who believed in me, the ones who did not and the ones who simply shook their heads yet encouraged me as I spoke about my crazy dreams for the future.

Thank you mom for always believing in me... I'm starting to "get it."

Thank you dad for the discipline and love you showed in your unique way.

Thank you to all who have touched my life whether consciously or unwittingly including the CC and the others who may no longer be with us in the physical world.

To my local heroes and supporters, you know who you are. You have my heartfelt gratitude.

Leanne, I love you, even though I don't say it enough.

The journey continues . . .

Table of Contents

Introduction

This story is fictional yet inspired by true events. Events have been modified for dramatic effect. Characters are fictional and any resemblance to a real person is purely coincidental. The political backdrop is real and based on actual historical events. The cruelty and hardships depicted were and still are real for the people of South Africa. I've kept the political facts intact since no writer could imagine the cruelty that actually occurred. I salute all my brothers and sisters fighting for justice and equality around the globe including my homeland, South Africa.

Live the principles in this book and teach it to others, especially your children, rather than letting it become just another book on your shelf. Change starts from within regardless of whether your fight is political, religious or personal.

Your Mindset truly does Determine your Outcome.

Chapter 1 ~ The Outcome

I put my arm around her and looked up as the bright flash from a camera blinded us. There was hardly time to get my eyes refocused when someone else took her place and posed with me for a photo and a hug. My cousins, *the cousins*, were there too and each waited their turn to wish me well on my journey. The terminal was full and I was pleasantly surprised at how many people had showed up to say goodbye. I was glad mom had insisted that we tell everyone the flight was three hours before the actual departure time or I would never make it.

"Here you go, more cookies for you. Do you have room in your carry-on bag?" I heard someone ask.

"I don't know. It's over there next to dad. I'll be back in a few minutes," I said and walked toward the airport bathroom.
I had to get away from my large, loving extended family to let this all sink in. This was it, I was really leaving and it was really, truly happening. I took my time washing my hands and spent a few extra minutes looking at the confident person staring back at me in the mirror. "What a journey you've had so far, what a journey," I said to my reflection when I heard my name being called. My little cousin was calling my name and had come running in to find me.

"Come, come. Grandma is looking for you," he squealed as he led me out of the bathroom and back to the waiting crowd.
I felt a strong tug on my shoulder and as I turned he gave me a big hug and flashed his broad smile.

"Hello my brother. Have a safe flight and study hard. Remember your roots as you share all that you have learned with the world." I smiled and squeezed him harder.

He hugged me tightly. "Hamba Kakushle (go well) my brother, Hamba Kakushle."

"I will. Thank you again for all that you've done for me. I will remember all that you…" My impatient cousin tugging on my sleeve interrupted me. "Come on, let's go."

I returned to my family gathered at the departure gate and looked around for grandma. She was much shorter than I was and I bent down to give her a hug.

I felt a tissue wipe my tears. It was mom waiting for another hug. I hugged her tightly and held her for a long time. She was crying and whispering words of love and encouragement as she held me tightly, not wanting to let go.

"Hurry up, it's time to board. Didn't you hear the announcement?" my annoyingly punctual aunt asked out loud.

I looked around to start gathering my bags but dad had already rounded them up and was walking toward the security gate.

I gave a few more quick hugs to those who were close by, said a loud goodbye and waved to everyone before joining dad for the short walk to the checkpoint where he had to stop and I had to keep going. He gave me his final words of wisdom and a hug as he said goodbye.

"Thanks dad. Yes, I will be careful. I will call when I get there. Reverse the charges, I know."

He had tears in his eyes as he handed me my backpack and carry-on bag. I turned away to wave to everyone one last time before I would be out of sight. As I waved, I smiled at what I saw beyond the family group, close to the exit door leading to the parking lot. Andrew was speaking to Peter to whom I had introduced him earlier.

I reached inside my jacket pocket for my boarding pass and passport. My hand brushed against a padded envelope that I didn't remember putting in there. The envelope, stuffed with cash, was from Andrew. He must have slid it in when he hugged me earlier.

I spotted a deli and stopped to make a quick purchase as I heard the announcement about my flight in the departure hall again.

The woman's voice was friendly and pleasant on the airport speaker – a far cry from the booming voice over the megaphone that had started me on this strange quest, culminating in me now boarding this flight. I boarded the plane ready for a new adventure. It was my first international flight and I was nervous and excited. Nervous and scared of what lay ahead of me, though not fearing for my life like I had been when this all started. I had my carry-on bag in one hand and a tuna sandwich in the other.

I had learned so much in such a short time, yet I vividly remember the day, *the very moment* that started it all.

Chapter 2 ~ My Awakening

"This is an illegal gathering!" the booming voice announced over the megaphone. "Disperse or we will be forced to take action."

I stopped singing and looked up to see army vehicles roll in and surround the school. The soldiers piled out and stood in formation with their weapons drawn, pointing directly at us.

This could not be happening I thought to myself. This could not be happening at my school. We were simply singing songs out here and not hurting anyone. This only happened on television in cities far away from me, not at my own school. I knew the next step would be teargas, followed by a wall of soldiers in riot gear charging in, beating people into submission and dragging them off to jail. At least that's what the politically involved teachers and students had said.

The seriousness of the situation set in when the megaphone squeaked again and the order was repeated. "This is an illegal gathering, disperse immediately or we will be forced to take action." This time his tone was more serious. Something big was about to happen here. These soldiers were trained killing machines and were hungry for action.

All they needed from any one of us was a reason for the order to be given so they could satisfy their need to fire.

It was a Friday afternoon and I was in a group of about two dozen students standing outside the classroom singing political freedom songs. I could feel the tension in the air and the seconds seemed like hours as time slowed down in my mind. My heart was pounding and my breathing was shallow even though my chest was heaving.

I fought the urge to run and stood as still as I could, watching and waiting for someone else to make the next move. My mind was racing yet I had no clear thoughts. If I moved it could be mistaken as provocation for them to take action.

I looked around. Nobody else had moved either. Even the soldiers in their full riot gear seemed frozen in time like the toy soldiers I played with as a child. One foot forward, chin slightly raised to see under the helmet and the handle of their weapon pressed firmly against their shoulder in the firing position.

Their eyes were the only things that made them human.

Their blinking eyes were real - focused and intent staring at us just waiting to go into action, unlike my dull, lifeless green toy soldiers at home.

The soldiers in full riot gear looked like new recruits, some only slightly older than me and just as nervous I was. For the first time in my young life I was staring down the business end of an automatic weapon.

Never in my life had I ever been this afraid. This was real. I could be dead in a few minutes. It was a paralyzing feeling. I knew deep down inside that if I lived, I would remember this moment for the rest of my life.

"Wait, captain wait. These children are just doing some harmless singing," I heard someone say. It was Mr. Phillips, a white biology teacher who had been at our school for years.

He had both his hands up in front of him, palms facing forward, as he stepped in front of us and spoke directly to the captain.

"They are leaving right now, is that alright sir?" He asked in English then repeated the question in Afrikaans.

The captain stared at him, then at us then back at Mr. Phillips.

"Are you part of this rally?" he asked in his thick Afrikaner accent, "part of these political troublemakers?" English was not his first language and he switched to Afrikaans when he spoke again.

"Get these people to leave right now. At once."
"Ja meneer (yes sir)" Mr. Phillips replied and turned to face us.

"Start at end of the line over here and leave slowly in that direction," he said pointing to the student closest to the captain and directing us to vacate the premises.

I nervously stepped in place as I impatiently waited for my turn to leave.

As soon as I was out of sight I ran. I ran like I had never run before because I felt like my life depended on it. I kept looking back to make sure I was not being followed as I headed home.

It was April of 1985 in Cape Town, South Africa and I was a sixteen-year old 'coloured boy' four months into my senior year of high school. The school year had started off with uncertainty due to the changing political climate in the country.

The winds of change had been blowing for some time and had now reached the school system. Students across the country had started standing up for the cause.

The CAUSE was a political one – equal rights and freedom for all citizens. The rest of the world had been paying attention to South Africa for many years and was putting pressure on the government of my country and its decades old Apartheid regime.

Many years of disinvestments, sanctions and trade embargos had affected the economy and were now influencing the political arena as well. Television shows had many not-so-subtle posters in their scenes that said "Free South Africa", "End Apartheid" or "Free Mandela" and protests were being staged outside South African embassies and consulates around the world.

The world was carefully watching us, especially since next year marked the tenth anniversary of the Soweto uprising in 1976. No one wanted to see a repeat of that event or the resultant high number of deaths. The whole political involvement at school had started slowly with students and teachers giving speeches during our lunch hour. There were about ten of them who would take turns updating us on what was happening politically around the country.

Our principal, Mr. Petersen, allowed peaceful 'protests' on the school grounds during lunch hour and after school around 2:30 p.m.

'Protests' being a relative term since to me it simply meant a reason to stay after school hanging out with the other seniors, listening to political rhetoric and singing along to songs I didn't even know the words to.

It seemed like harmless fun since the only 'audience' for these protests were other students leaving to go home who were either too young or too distracted to even notice what us seniors were doing.

Students would gather in the schoolyard and speak out about how our education was inferior to whites and how we lacked modern equipment and supplies in our school.

Despite this bleak description, my school, a 'coloured' school, was extremely progressive and ahead of its time in many ways. White teachers willingly came to teach here with their black and coloured colleagues. We were taught to see each other as equals and accepted the challenges, cultural diversity and personalities of one another respectfully…well about as respectful as teenagers could be.

My school quietly welcomed black students and offered Xhosa, a black language, as part of the regular curriculum.

I made it home and collapsed on my bed, my heart and mind racing. This was the scariest experience of my life. *I had faced and escaped death.*

I didn't know what to do. Should I go back to school and get involved again or just stay in the safety of my home? Fortunately I had three weeks of Easter break ahead of me. There were only three more school days before the term ended.

Our school year runs from January to December with a few weeks off in April and September as well as a month off in June after we take our mid-year exams. Final exams for us seniors would be in late November instead of the usual December exams before we take our summer break. Results for the final exams arrive in the mail about ten days later then gets printed in the newspaper just before Christmas. Summer vacation gives you time to relax in the sun so you can start the New Year refreshed and relaxed.

I knew I had to start getting serious about my studies and prepare for midterms in June and finals if I wanted to get out of high school. I had to find a way to get better organized and more focused on my schoolwork and facing death before graduation was not part of my plan for my senior year.

Not that I didn't want to do better. I was constantly struggling with schoolwork and it was not for lack of trying. On the contrary, I loved reading and learning new things and was always checking out books from the local public library on many eclectic subjects.

By age 12, I could amaze my family and friends with magic tricks, had spent countless hours with my microscope thanks to the sacrifice of many insects, had memorized all kinds of random, trivial facts and could name almost every bone and major muscle group in the human body.

Such were the varied topics I enjoyed learning about and I excelled in them as I soaked in all the information. Even now as a senior I would spend hours at the library, which was close to school and only a few blocks from home, after school and after finishing my chores at home. In fact, my favorite uncle who visited almost every Sunday would always ask me questions on random topics and enjoyed seeing my face light up as I went into a long explanation if I knew about his chosen topic.

He jokingly called me "doc" because to him I represented a fountain of knowledge.

"You know so much, someday you'll really be a doc, doc," he would say as he smiled and walked away shaking his head after I had given him a detailed and obscure answer to his question. I think my thick spectacles and furrowed brow contributed to the image as I contemplated my answers.

I could spend many hours at the library and enjoyed the fact that stillness was enforced on the patrons. At the library I could find a book on any topic I wished to study and escape from the rigid subjects I was forced to study in school. I could simply walk over to a shelf and in minutes be transported to any country, culture or topic in the world. I felt completely in charge of my life when I stepped into the library and gazed upon the myriads of choices available to me.

Not that I was terrible at school. I just didn't seem to fit in with my classmates. I had started first grade earlier than most and was always the youngest in my class. Even now as a senior, I was two years younger than everyone else and a model student with no behavioral issues except for my grades. The only subjects I excelled in were biology, physics and language – I took Xhosa in school so I could communicate in a black language.

To the outside world, I appeared to be an intelligent, smart young man; inwardly I struggled. Only my immediate family knew how much trouble I was having. In fact, any school project that required a lot of reading and writing followed by a test gave me trouble.

I caught my breath and was thinking about how and why I was involved in the rally in the first place. It wasn't really a conscious, deliberate decision. I was only present to be there with my fellow seniors in a cause that seemed important to them.

I stayed out of trouble and especially stayed out of politics. As a 'boy of colour' I was content in my world, simply accepting the way things were and doing my best to survive. The law of the land dictated where we could live, how we should live and even which door to use when entering a building, bus or train. On the train, the first few coaches were reserved for whites only and labeled 'first class', while the rear coaches labeled 'third class' were for us non-whites. Non-white is a broad section of the population and included Indians, Coloureds and Blacks. You obeyed authority without question regardless of whether you agreed with the policy.

The white minority was in power and your life was in their hands. The blacks were really nothing more than slaves and had to carry documentation at all times. They were not stuck on the plantation like they were in America, however they were at the mercy of the white man. It was nothing new. It had been that way in America for years and was still that way here in South Africa. If you caused trouble you were jailed or killed and if you remained subservient you would be treated well and given a chance to move ahead.

Of course moving ahead was a relative term since non-whites were rarely allowed to advance to management positions. There was a strange symbiosis in play with the black and coloured men taking the jobs requiring hard labor and the women taking the jobs as cooks and cleaners in the house of the white man and occasionally the wealthy black, indian & coloured people too. Politically we were seen as animals anyway, animals who should always be obedient to their masters.

For the first time in my sheltered life the reality of my race, the colour of my skin and how much I was being oppressed hit me. I was and always would be seen as a coloured boy.

Great realization I thought to myself, what are you going to do? Stay home or get involved in politics and face the consequences?

And more importantly - Was this CAUSE worth dying for? I was caught between two worlds, the world of being comfortable and staying in denial or the new world that was unfolding with this realization.

That was the ultimate question. I had heard many unbelievable stories during the lunchtime and after school speeches. The speeches were both interesting and informative. I learnt about the long history of the political parties in South Africa, the history of the British versus the Dutch and the black political movement's unsuccessful attempts against the government dating back to the early '60s.

The great victory for the current regime was the successful arrest and incarceration of ten leaders of the banned political party, ANC (African National Congress), including Nelson Mandela. They were charged and eventually convicted of terrorism during the Rivonia Trial in 1964. Due to the worldwide objection and outcry, the death sentences were changed to life in prison for the eight who were finally convicted.

Now over twenty years later history was repeating itself on the political front. I would hear about people of all ages being arrested around the country for their political involvement and how they were being held in detention indefinitely without trial. Even children were being arrested without their parents being notified for days, sometimes months.

We were approaching the tenth anniversary of the Soweto uprising and tensions were high. During one of the presentations the story of what had occurred on that day was told.

The Soweto uprising started as a peaceful outdoor protest on June 16th 1976 against a law that had been passed the previous year. The law required that all schools, including black schools use Afrikaans as well as English as languages of instruction. Afrikaans, which was seen as the language of the white oppressor was mandated for all black students despite an earlier poll that showed 98% against the idea.

The protest in Soweto, close to Johannesburg, was intended to be a peaceful gathering. Students of all ages joined by teachers would show solidarity against this law by peacefully marching through the streets and convening at one chosen school.

The police who had prior knowledge of this event barricaded and closed some roads along the route. The crowd grew to over eight thousand people. They had been warned that this may occur and asked not to provoke the authorities. Encountering the armed police at a closed street, the crowd started moving away to take another route to their destination.

A policeman at the scene, claiming that the students had started throwing stones at them, drew his handgun and fired directly into the crowd. Chaos ensued as the crowd panicked and started running in all directions. That first shot was taken as permission to fire and more policemen started firing randomly into the crowd.

This led to the angry crowd then hurling stones at the police. Riot police using bullets and teargas closed in to control the large crowd. The army was called in to help as things quickly got out of control and clashes continued into the night.

The pandemonium left over six hundred dead, including young students and over a thousand injured. Exact numbers could not be confirmed since many wounds were not recorded for fear of repercussions from the police. The true story of how and why everything occurred will never be known.

What is known is that this event marked a turning point for South Africa and made the world start paying attention to what was happening in the country.

American and European companies started disinvesting, leaving the country and the economy on a downward spiral. A worldwide group consciousness and awareness of the atrocities in South Africa as well many other countries had formed and now, ten years later had reached our shores and stirred the hearts and minds of all South Africans that a change of some sort was necessary. Change had always been feared since history showed that implosion, destruction and civil war were the typical net results of political upheaval.

As bad as the stories were, they were only stories and did not affect me personally. Of course I felt bad for those involved but there was nothing *I* could do about it.

I didn't know that my school had been under surveillance for months because some teachers and students at our school were considered political instigators by the authorities. The seriousness of our actions became very clear to me when I faced the soldiers after what I had considered a harmless activity at school.

I had a restless night as the events of the day kept replaying in my head. The vision of the soldiers with their burning eyes and weapons pointing at me kept jarring me awake throughout the night. I must have fallen asleep at some point because I was awakened first by mom then by dad as they came in to say goodbye on their way to work.

Chapter 3 ~ My First Encounter

It was Saturday and I had chores to do. I reluctantly did them even though I couldn't really concentrate on what I was doing. After mowing the lawn and finishing my other chores, I knew I would have the afternoon to myself.

I had to clear my head and I knew exactly where I could go to do that - the public library. It was the only place where the world was literally at my fingertips. Only this time I was going there to run away from my problems and get lost in a novel where I could relate to the hero or, perhaps more accurately this time, relate to the poor soul in the book whose life was in turmoil like mine.

I finished my chores and headed to the library. Little did I know that this trip to the library was the start of a journey that would take me thousands of kilometres away from Cape Town.

Proceeding up the path to the front door of the library, I passed a gardener pruning the bushes along the walkway in the hot sun. He was a tall man with big hands holding the pruning shears. I had never seen him before and couldn't help but smile as I heard him whistling while he cheerfully gyrated in a mock dance with the bush he was trimming. He moved gracefully even with his work boots on. I was surprised to see him wearing an American style baseball cap and blue jeans instead of overalls, as I would have expected.

He stopped momentarily and nodded to me as I passed him. How fortunate he was not to have my life I thought - the miserable, confused life of a teenager who had just faced death.

"Kunjani? (How are you?)" I said as I walked by.

"Ndiphilile namhlanje (I am well today)" he answered.

"Uyasithetha isiXhosa? (Do you speak Xhosa?)," he asked.

"Ewe, ndisifunde esikolweni (yes, I am learning it at school)."

"Wait" he said switching to English. "Come over for a minute, I needing your help with something. You know anything about gardening?"

I resisted the urge to correct his grammar. "*I need* not needing and its *do you know*, not you know," I thought to myself as I paused and turned to face him. He was not the type of person I would typically take the time to chat with. I briefly wondered why he would need my help but decided to be polite and at least listen to him instead of letting him know that I was not in the mood to be sociable. I was here to escape from my present situation in life with a mindless novel.

"Sorry, I have to get going. I have to get a book for school." I lied then turned to walk back toward the library.

"It's not in there," he said pointing to the library. "Is here not here," he pointed to his heart then to his head. "The answer is not in the building. Come, come."

I stopped in mid-stride and turned to face him again. I wasn't sure whether I should smile and walk away or get sucked in to his conversation. Was he serious or simply teasing a teenager on a Saturday afternoon. What a strange thing to say to me, or to anyone for that matter. Admittedly though, I was curious. What had made him say what he said? I wasn't quite sure if he was being rude or if he routinely made such quizzical statements to all the patrons. I decided to pry a little further before I continued my mission.

"What's your name?" I asked, "and what are you talking about?"

"My name doesn't matter, Andrew if it makes you feel important little man. "

What a jerk, I thought, did he just call me "little man." How dare this uneducated gardener speak to me in this way? He didn't know me; I was simply being polite and making conversation. I knew it was just a fluke that what he said triggered a reaction in me. I was on edge after yesterday's near-death experience. Well! I wasn't a fool and I refused to get involved in his silly game. I had faced death and I wasn't going to let a stupid gardener ruin my mood even further.

"What do you mean, if it makes me feel important little man?"

"You know what I means," he said snidely.

Another grammatical error I thought and once again stopped myself from correcting him.

"Nice talking to you Andrew." I snipped and turned to walk away. "Sorry I can't help you."

"Then at least whistle," he said. "You can at least pretend to be happy then. It is impossible to whistle while you are sad or upset…or confused? If you can't help me at least help yourself for a few minutes." He started whistling as he turned his back to me and went back to pruning the bushes.

Shaking my head and angry for letting him upset me, I entered my intended sanctuary. I started in the non-fiction section, which I knew very well, then changed my mind. I was here for a novel, a mindless book to help me escape and after my tiff with Andrew I really didn't want to learn anything right now.

I walked past the magazine racks and the romance novel section and headed for the hardcovers. Using my index finger I skimmed the titles on the shelf and quickly moved across and down the selections. Nothing jumped out at me as I moved from shelf to shelf. Nothing looked interesting, nothing at all. With so many choices there had to be something here to help me fulfill my mission. All these books available to me yet not one peaked my interest this time. It shouldn't have been this difficult to find something.

Andrew was still on my mind. How dare he speak to me that way? He didn't know me. I was just being polite when I said hello. Was it a lack of suitable titles or Andrew's comment that was distracting me?

I headed for the periodicals. Perhaps reading about some celebrity's problem would be mindless enough.

"No, no, nope" I muttered audibly as I went from magazine to magazine. Nothing looked interesting here either.

How dare he speak to me that way, he didn't know me, the thought returned. Andrew, the damn gardener was in my head again. I had to go find him and ask him what he meant. I was not going to let him get to me like this.

I walked outside to find him. I headed back to the bushes at the end of the walkway where I had first encountered Andrew. Even though I was angry, I had to admit that he had done a great job. He had trimmed them on top and sheared the sides straight down. The three bushes on either side of the walkway by the front gate looked like a welcoming committee standing at attention as you entered the property. Andrew wasn't there and I didn't see him as I looked around. Walking around to the side of the building I spotted him.

He was down on his knees scooping fertilizer and soil from a bucket next to him and packing it around the flowers at the edge of the flowerbed. The flowers were part of a larger group that formed a labyrinth with a concrete walkway through to a circular area with benches under the trees. This area was popular with the older adults who would check out two or three books at a time then sit under the shade of the trees to read instead of going home right away.

All the benches were occupied. The autumn weather had been unusually warm and everyone was fully enjoying the sunshine before the rainy days of winter in June.

I walked over to Andrew who was on his knees turned away from me. As I came closer I was surprised to hear his voice. He was speaking to the flowers. He would lovingly speak to a flower as his gloved hands gently packed dirt and fertilizer around the base. Then he would say thank you and move to the next flower while still on his knees speaking softly.

I watched him for a few minutes and approached him just as he was finishing the last one in the row.

"Andrew", I said softly as I put my hand on his shoulder. He looked up at me and smiled.

"Are you ready?" he said with a twinkle in his eye. "Are you ready my brother?"

Chapter 4 ~ The Lessons Begin

I was caught off guard. What a strange opening statement. Was I ready for what?

"Excuse me? Am I ready for what? I was coming to ask you what you meant earlier."

"In time, my brother, in time. All the answers will come to you. The main question is are you ready? Well! Are you?"

I was intrigued; he wants to continue playing this game. O.K. pal, you have no idea who you are dealing with. This is an easy game to win when you have a high school senior versus an uneducated gardener. This would be too easy. I had nothing to lose by hearing what a gardener had to say. Perhaps he would teach me about gardening. Plants and flowers did not usually peak my interest and I wouldn't typically waste time reading a book on it so this would be a good lesson anyway. I could always walk away when I got bored; which I was certain wouldn't take very long. I had a few hours to spare on a Saturday afternoon so why the heck not learn something about gardening today.

I decided to take the bait, for now. "OK, sure, I'm ready." "I hope so," he said sarcastically, "we'll know soon enough. Come with me my brother."

I helped him pack up the supplies he had been using for the flowers and followed him to the back of the main library building. We stopped at a steel door with a large padlock securing it.

He put down the buckets he had been carrying and reached for keys that were attached to his belt. The large bunch of keys was clipped to a loop in his pants and secured to his belt with a retractable cord.

I watched the cord stretch from his belt as he quickly found the right key, unlocked the padlock and opened the door.

He flipped a light switch as we entered and I looked around the room. We were in a well-lit storage room with a stale, musty smell. The room had two racks with three shelves along one wall and two peg boards along the other. I followed him to one corner where he returned the garden supplies to the shelf.

I was surprised to see how neat the room was kept. The garden supplies had a rack of their own where the supplies were arranged by use. The bag of fertilizer and soil went on the bottom shelf, seeds and gloves were on the middle shelf and various sprays sat on the top shelf. A meticulously clean push mower sat next to the garden shelf. Next to the garden rack a pegboard was nailed to the wall where Andrew had neatly hung all the garden tools.

Across from the garden rack was the cleaning rack. Buckets and new mop heads and rags lined the bottom shelf, three types of plungers and toilet brushes were on the middle shelf and cleaning sprays and supplies lined the top shelf.

On the pegboard next to the garden rack hung a variety of tools from hammers to brooms. A toolbox, a tool belt and two vacuum cleaners sat below the pegboard.

Andrew walked over to the pegboard and retrieved two brooms then gestured for me to follow him outside. We stopped just long enough for him to close the door and replace the padlock then we walked around the building to the walkway at the main entrance.

"Time to clean" he said as he pointed to the walkway. "No talking, only sweeping. We start here at the gate all the way to the building. Sweep the walkway and sweep your mind at the same time. There's a lot in there getting in the way, so take your time. Look out for the dirt and the cobwebs and the people. Even at your age, there's a lot in there," he repeated pointing to my head.

As he said the word 'people' he handed me a broom and started sweeping the walkway behind some patrons who had just entered.

I took the broom without argument and followed his lead. He started at the midpoint of the walkway on the right side and swept out to the edge. He pointed to the unswept side and kept going.

I started next to him on the left and swept outward to the edge of the walkway. Together we swept, only stopping to let people walk by as they entered or left the library.

The varied responses I received from the crowd were both unexpected and surprising. Some people would wait for me to finish then quietly walk by behind me. Others would offer an "excuse me" and proceed without waiting for me to acknowledge them. Some simply kept walking without even looking at me and glared at me if I happened to swipe their shoes when they walked by.

Andrew just kept sweeping and whistling, away in his own world. He didn't seem as aware of all the reactions as I was. Besides their actions I also started noticing the looks I was getting. Some would smile, nod and politely walk by. Some people would look down at me as if what I was doing was beneath them while others would say thank you as they smiled at us. These varied responses to my sweeping came from people of all ages, gender and race.

"Did you clean your mind?" Andrew asked when we were done.

"Uh, not really," I said. "I was too busy getting treated like the dirt I was sweeping, although there were some nice people too. I couldn't focus on myself when I kept getting in the way of everyone else."

"I didn't get in their way," he answered quickly.

"You have just learned to ignore them," I answered as I recalled some of the rude responses.

He gave a smug smile. "No, I was focused on sweeping, treating the walkway, the broom and the people with respect. When you work from inside yourself, you let yourself out. When you look outside, you let the people in. Only you have the power to keep people out or to let them in. When your mind is full you get confused. Besides, you have more sweeping to do, in here."

He pointed to my head again as he continued.

"Clean up in there and you won't end up sweeping the walkway of a library for the rest of your life. When you sweep clean your mind, get rid of the dirt in there, you can have a clean mind for good things to enter. Never mind what people say to you or do to you, with a clean mind you get to start over every time.

People come here to read and to learn while I take care of the building that keeps them smart. I'm the maintenance man and the gardener. If only they knew that a man who can hardly read is taking care of their library."

I looked at him in surprise. Surprised to hear how me helping him sweep the sidewalk had turned into a philosophical lesson about life, not the simple gardening lesson I had expected.

"OK," I answered, wanting to hear more, "I get it. How do I clean my mind?"

"Start by acknowledging that your mind needs cleaning. If you choose to ignore this fact then you are choosing to remain where you are." He looked directly into my eyes to make sure I was listening before he continued.

"There are a few categories of people in this world, those who know that they are stuck and those who don't know. There are also people who know that they are stuck yet refuse to change or don't know how to change so they accept where they are and get comfortable being average. Even when a solution is offered to them they are scared to take a chance and to lose what little they already have. Being comfortable is easy; it requires no effort and is a powerful reason to remain stuck. They are so comfortable being average and ordinary that any deviation from their 'norm' scares them. Improving yourself is not an easy thing to do – it wasn't meant to be easy. Start by being aware of how many thoughts you have every day that keep you stuck. How often do you turn away from something because it requires effort and you talk yourself out of a new experience? You will be surprised my brother at how much our minds keep us stuck. Keep sweeping and come back when you have more space in there."

He took the broom from me, "Thank you for helping me, I'll see you soon my brother" and walked toward the library building without saying another word. I took this as my cue that the lesson was over for the day.

"Nice to meet you Andrew. Sala Kakushle (stay well)."
I called after him as he quickly walked off toward the storage room.

Chapter 5 ~ My Favorite Uncle

Mom and dad were just getting home when I walked in. Dad and I went out for lawn inspection as he insisted on doing every week after I had mowed. I knew what to expect. It was never good enough. He proceeded to tell me what I had done wrong and how to fix it the next time I mowed. I half listened to his rehashed advice then went inside to help prepare supper. I ate in silence as my mind kept going over what I had learned from Andrew. I declined to share what I was thinking when mom pointed out that I seemed distant and occupied during the meal.

"Sorry mom," was all I muttered as I continued pondering my strange day and my even stranger new friend named Andrew.

Sunday started off early with my uncle stopping by for a visit earlier than usual and staying until lunchtime. My uncle was a businessman who worked all the time yet would regularly visit us on Sundays. He came for lunch almost every Sunday since it was the only day that his wife didn't cook. She would take my two cousins to see her parents and spend the day with them.

My uncle owned three mini mart grocery stores and spent his days traveling between them delivering supplies and orders. He was preparing his two boys to take over the stores, especially the older of the two who was 4 years my senior. His brother, though two years older than me was a senior in high school too. My uncle had been grooming his eldest son for ownership and management of the main store by having him take business and management courses at the local college a few nights a week.

It was interesting to me how much I cared for this man yet could not stand being around his sons. I think it was because of his work ethic and his down-to-earth attitude.

He had worked hard all his life saving his money while he was on the police force and in the army. After he left the army he made some wise investments with his army buddies that paid off better than expected and gave him the seed money to start his first store. He opened his first store in a low-income area of Cape Town and did well in the community. He developed a reputation for being fair to his employees and his customers, treating everyone equally and rarely turned anyone away from the store. I had heard many stories of him giving families extra groceries when they didn't have enough money.

His business grew quickly and within a few years he had opened a second then a third store in other low income areas. He worked hard and he played hard as well. Mom and dad had mentioned in passing conversation to my brother and I how well he was doing financially due to his savvy business acumen yet he never flaunted his wealth. He drove a truck every day and only drove his luxury vehicle on Sunday when he came to visit. I was more excited than he was and asked him to take us for a ride when he first showed up with it a few years ago. He obliged and simply drove us around the neighborhood for a few minutes without bragging about all the features in his new vehicle. Unfortunately these traits were not passed along to his children.

His wife was not well liked. The whole family believed that she had only married him for his money. She was not very sociable and stayed away from family gatherings. Despite her wealth she would always be on the lookout for sales and coupons, even driving out of her way to save a few cents on groceries. I would overhear my uncle complain to mom about how she would spend more in fuel than she would save as a result of her store hopping, coupon clipper habit.

"I like a good deal too but jeez, she's ridiculous with it. It's not like we don't have the money for groceries. I'd rather eat what we stock in the store than some of the things she buys on sale."

Due to my uncles hectic work schedule she was the one who spent the most time with the boys as they were growing up and had turned them into snobs.

My cousins would get whatever they asked for and were always the first to get the latest and the greatest fashions and gadgets on the market. In fact they were such snobs that they refused to be seen in our neighborhood and would hardly come visit. They refused to park their expensive cars in our driveway and on the rare occasions they were forced to be at our house, would make a big production of locking their cars and loudly setting the car alarm while it sat in the driveway. My uncle would shrug off their attitudes and showed his love for his brother's family by spending Sundays with us whenever he could. Besides, he loved seeing the new magic tricks I was constantly learning and always made me feel good when I put on a show for him.

"Any new tricks to show me doc," he would ask after giving me a bear hug when he came to visit. If I had something new to show him, he would ask for a show and pretend not to notice when I accidentally goofed the trick.

At school on Monday I heard that all political activities were cancelled and would not resume until we came back from our Easter break. All around the country though, the political activities were increasing and now dozens of arrests, including students were being made daily. I focused on getting my schoolwork done and didn't get a chance to visit Andrew again. I didn't have to though. His words and his simple lesson of sweeping had made an impact on me.

I started paying more attention to my thoughts during the Easter break. Without the busyness of school I found that my mind was still very noisy and to my surprise I realized that it started from the moment I awakened to the time I went to bed.

As if that wasn't enough, my tossing and turning coupled with crazy, vivid dreams made me realize that my noisy mind didn't even turn off at night. I had not shared any of this with my family although Mom commented that I seemed more occupied than usual for someone who was on school break.

My uncle offered me a job for the holidays at the main store. I gladly accepted the chance to get out of the house and make some money. I was two years away from driving age so I took the train to and from work during the week and he picked me up on Fridays and Saturdays. I enjoyed working with him because he spent extra time with me when he was at my location.

He came to visit the store on my first day there and called me into his office at lunchtime. He handed me two twenties and sent me to the deli that was a few stores down "two tuna sandwiches, orange juice for me and whatever you want to drink." When I returned with his meal he was waiting at his desk. I put everything down in front of him and handed him his change. He didn't take it and commented on my choice of drink instead.

"Your change sir," I said placing it on his desk.
"Keep it," he smiled, "call it a delivery charge. Have a seat," he said as he handed me one of the tuna sandwiches.

"Thank you very much," I answered as I sat down and took the sandwich. I didn't have the heart to tell him that I didn't like tuna, especially since he had let me keep the rather substantial amount of change.

"Anything new and exciting in your life that I should know about?" he asked as I sat across from him at his desk.

"Not really," I replied. I spoke about the store while he listened intently, briefly commenting between bites as I chatted.

As we finished eating, he arose and cleared away the wrappers.

"OK, back to work for both of us. Anything else before I go?"

"No sir," I answered, "and thank you for lunch."
I cared deeply for this man and was extremely grateful to him for many reasons. Not simply for the food, but for keeping me company and checking on me at my first real job. We had a great conversation and he had listened to me when I spoke. My own dad had never sat down with me like this for a friendly conversation over lunch.

"No problem, take care of the store. See you soon."

I returned to work elated and happy. I was touched by his gesture of coming to check on me on my first day. This was his first and busiest store and it kept me pretty occupied. He had instructed my cousin to let me leave early enough to catch the train and be home before dark. My first day was soon done and I felt good.

Two days later he returned at lunchtime and repeated the process, including letting me keeping the change again and eating with him at his desk. I soon realized that it was his way of letting me know how much he cared about me while it also gave him a sneaky way to give me extra money.

By the following week I had figured out his routine and found myself looking forward to his visits. Admittedly, I had also learned to love tuna sandwiches as much as he did. This routine continued for all three weeks of my time at the store. Even though I was busy at work my mind was constantly racing yet none of it made sense to me.

Andrew was right, I had many thoughts throughout the day that were negative and I couldn't seem to stop them. I had to go see him again so he could shed some light on what I was experiencing.

I was ready leave the working world and get back to school so I could focus on graduating.

Chapter 6 ~ Label Blinders

I finally had a chance to get away on the last day of vacation. It was Sunday and I knew my uncle would not be visiting. I finished my chores at home as quickly as I could and ran to the library to go see my new friend. It was early in the afternoon when I entered the gate to the library. I stopped momentarily to admire the trimmed bushes that Andrew had obviously recently done.

I spotted him at the flowerbeds on the side of the building. He was on his knees again speaking to the flowers as I approached him. How ironic I thought, this is where the adventure had begun.

"Andrew" I called to him as I came up behind him. "I have many questions for you, can we chat while you work"

"Kunjani? (How are you?) my brother," he asked as he turned to see who had been calling him.

A smile spread across his face and his eyes sparkled just a little more than usual when he recognized me.

"My brother, it's been a while. Good to see you again."

"Good to see you too, Andrew. Can you chat while you work?"

"No, I can chat while *we* work" he said jokingly, "You can help me. Are you ready? Grab some gloves and help me feed the flowers," he said pointing to the rubber garden gloves next to him.

I pulled the gloves on quickly and sat down next to him. I took a handful of the fertilizer/soil mix from the bucket, quickly packed it around a flower then moved to the next one. This was easy, I thought. This shouldn't take long at all.

Was I ready? What a joke. I had done four flowers when I realized that he had not moved and was simply staring at me.

"What's the matter? I'm doing what you were doing. Let's get it done so we can move on."

"You are not going to make this easy are you? You said you were ready."

"Well, I'm not a gardener you know but this isn't hard to do. OK, tell me more about sweeping and clearing my mind. My mind has been racing since the last time we spoke."

He sighed and continued speaking as if I hadn't said a word.

"First step, slow down and focus completely on what you are doing. The flower is alive and she can feel you. Speak to her and let her know that you are feeding her with love and respect.

She will show you her gratitude when she grows tall and strong and show you her love with beautiful blossoms. If you learn to treat a flower with respect, you will treat yourself and others with respect too. You must, must, must appreciate every moment because when it's gone it's gone forever. Now come back here and do the first one again…with respect."

"It's only fertilizer, why waste time on it?

He smiled and repeated what he had said, "With respect my brother, with respect."

I felt foolish at first but I followed his advice. I watched him take his time and say a few words as he worked around each flower. He even packed the mixture lovingly around the base rather than haphazardly like I had done. By the time I had returned to the fourth flower a few minutes later I was following his routine. As I kept working my way around the flowerbed and the labyrinth, I started enjoying the procedure and took my time making each one better than the one before. I was relaxing and enjoying the time in the sun.

"Come," said a voice behind me.

Andrew had walked over to get my attention. I looked up and realized that we were done and he had already packed up all the supplies. It felt like I had been there longer than the thirty minutes that we had been working.

"Come" he said again, "we must continue."
I got up, stretched my legs and followed him around the building to the parking lot and over to a concrete bordered flowerbed.

There were three of them spaced across the parking lot all with their flowers still in bloom.

"More flowers to do. Take a deep breath and feel their love," he said and left me with the supplies.

"Wait a minute. I'm doing these by myself? I'm not getting paid to help you, you know. Besides, I wouldn't want a job as a gardener."

"Why not my brother? Do you not like the flowers and the trees? Are you too fragile to be in the sun? Are your high school hands too sensitive to respect these flowers? What is wrong with being a gardener?"

"You don't have many friends do you Andrew? You've just insulted me again and it's only the second time we've met. Good-bye, I'm done. I don't need to be insulted by you and I shouldn't have come back to bother you. Thanks but no thanks." I got up feeling hurt by someone I thought was a new friend and started to walk away. Just what I needed today, I mumbled under my breath...to be insulted by a gardener and to play with fertilizer on the last day of my vacation.

"Are you mad at me?" I heard Andrew ask. "Did I really insult you?"

"Yes I'm mad at you and you know you insulted me. I came back for answers not for insults from you. I should have known better, sorry I bothered you."

"When you look at me what do you see?" he asked quietly, breaking my train of thought.

"What do mean what do I see? I see you of course, so what?"

"Most people see a black gardener doing what is expected of a black man - manual labor. I am judged, even by you, by the color of my skin and by the type of work I am doing. It is assumed that I am not smart, yet with just a few words I can upset someone smart like you. You are in the high school down the road, yes?"

"Yes, so what? What does that have to do with you treating me like I'm the gardener, like I'm your slave?"

"You learn from books every day my brother. You memorize and you learn and you take tests from what you learn in the books. I learn from people, real people, not from books every day. When you pass the grades you move on to another subject forgetting what you have learned before. If you do remember, you have a hard time figuring out how what you know applies to real life.

In your mind you know so much more than I do, so why do you say that I insult you. I had to leave school in fifth grade to go find a job and now here I am years later. A black man doing what you think a black man should be doing – manual labor. When you see it, you relax because everything is all right in the world. You would look twice if you saw a white man in the garden, wouldn't you? To you, Mr. smart student, a gardener is a nobody right?"

"I'm sorry but I didn't mean to insult you."

"Sorry comes after you have said or done what you know you shouldn't have my brother. It is a word that comes so easily to some and yet so hard for others to utter. Sorry comes after you hurt someone intentionally because you think you are better than they are. I said what I said to shake up your mind not to insult you. You were hurtful in what you said to me weren't you? Here's the difference between you and me my brother. You learn from books, I learn from people. I don't talk good and I don't write good, but I learn good. When you learn only from books your brain gets full and you have no space to learn from people too. What you have my brother, is label blinders,"

"Label blinders? I've never heard of it. What are label blinders"?

"This means you give someone a label and with that label comes certain expectations. These labels come from childhood and we carry them with us for life. Some are good, most are bad."

"What do you mean? Please explain." I knew there was an important lesson coming and I started paying attention and letting my anger subside.

"I'll give you a few examples of things in your life that you do not even realize you had labeled. Are you ready?'

"That question again. What did you mean by it earlier when you asked if I was ready?"

"When you walked in here the first time you were so proud that you could greet me in my own language. Then, when you walk away you carry on with your life. Just because you can speak my language doesn't make you a Xhosa man just like me speaking English doesn't make me an English man. When you hear Xhosa you expect to see a black man, which is an accurate label.

When you see a group of black men standing on the street corner in the middle of the day, what is the label that goes with it?

"Trouble" I said before I could stop myself.

"Exactly. Your label says that they must be up to no good. When you see a group of children with backpacks what does your label say?"

"Students on their way to school."

"Right! Now let's go a little deeper. When you see group of men in suits what does your label say?"

"Businessmen of course."

"Good, now what if you see a black man in that group?"

"I would wonder what he was doing with them."

"Exactly! He would look out of place wouldn't he? Why is that? Because your label says that a black man cannot be a businessman in this country. Yes, there are a few of course but stay with me on this. There is a label that says a black man is not smart enough to vote or to have a good job. Labels are what we have been taught and what we have come to believe. This is how the government is keeping you and me in our places. We have believed the labels that we have been given. Even if there were no law, we would still believe that we were meant to stay small. Your labels keep you in prison. Our brothers who are being arrested for wanting to get rid of their labels are not the ones in prison; it's all of us out here who are walking around trapped by our labels living in the prison of our minds. Change the way you see things my brother and your life will change. It's not easy, but then again, it's not supposed to be easy. This is what I keep asking you, are you ready? Are you ready to be released from the prison of your mind?"

He put his hands on the side of my head and came nose to nose with me as he made the next statement.

"When you free yourself from your mental prison the way you see yourself and the way you see the world will change for sure.

The answers are inside of you and you will hear them when you learn to listen. Even simple things like placing fertilizer around the garden will be different when you are not trapped. Every moment of every day you and I have an opportunity to change a life. It may be your life, it may be my life or it may be the life of a stranger.

We have to take complete responsibility of this duty we have and take pride and honor in everything we do. Whether I am stocking the shelves, laying fertilizer or plunging toilets I am fully present in what I'm doing because I realize the long term effects that it has on me and on the world around me."

"Plunging toilets, are you serious?" I asked in an attempt to lighten the mood.

Andrew didn't flinch and kept speaking. "Yes, even plunging toilets. Some people think they are too good to do it.

There is no such thing; we are all human beings no matter what we look like on the outside. If you cannot take pride in that simple task then how can you take pride in anything else that you do? Every single thing and I do mean every single thing you do requires that you give it your best. Can you imagine what our world; no forget the world, what our country would be like if we all did that?"

He paused for a moment and I saw sadness in his eyes. "You are not your job my brother or your skin colour my brother or even the level of your education. There are many smart people who are still in prison in their minds no matter what their race or their degrees. They give you a label and with that label come certain behaviors, expectations and attitudes. I can give a broom to a professor or a doctor and have them help me sweep and as long as no one recognizes them they will get treated the same way that you did the other day.

"Labels and expectations are very strong and are taught to us at an early age. When you hear them all your life you start to believe it. Eventually you even come to expect the disrespect and attitudes that go with them. If the doctor kept playing janitor do you think he will accept them too?"

"I wouldn't think so. People will see that he's not a janitor, won't they?"

"You are not your education. You are not your job either. Be careful with what you are saying. People fall into a trap of believing that what they do defines who they are."

44

He paused briefly and took a deep breath before he passionately continued. His mind was rolling and he was sharing freely and openly from the heart. My mind was open and I was intently absorbing the wisdom and power of his words.

"This is why good people do bad things. They didn't start out as bad people yet they became that way because they believed the labels that they were given. The doctor in his office eventually believes that he has the power to cure people and develops an 'I'm-better-than-you attitude'. Yet, if that same person due to whatever reason has to be a janitor he will believe and act according to the label that goes with that job.

Our country has laws that keep us physically oppressed.

One day my brother, I don't know when but one day those laws will be gone. Do you think the people of this country will be better? No, they will still be oppressed.

It is worse to be mentally suppressed than physically oppressed.

"The great part is that we have choices, something that sets us humans apart from other animals. In your mind you can believe whatever you wish to believe, no matter what others say about you or how they treat you. Do you understand so far?"

"Um yes, yes I do. My label said that I had to get paid to help you and that I was too good to be gardener. Your label or lack of label says nobody is too good for anything and to do everything with pride. I would say I'm sorry but I know you won't accept my apology."

"It's not up to me. Is your apology good enough to make up for your thinking? You said out loud what you were thinking before you could stop yourself. Do you realize that others act on their negative thoughts without realizing what they are doing or even worse, why they are doing it? These are not thoughts my brother, this is programming. I'll leave that for another day though. It's getting late and I need to get these flowers done before the sun goes down."

"No problem, I'm here to help." I reached down, grabbed the gloves and knelt down in the flowerbed. I focused on each flower and treated them with respect while I considered what Andrew had just taught me.

I had many thoughts going through my mind, this time not thoughts of death but thoughts of labels and how a simple greeting a few weeks ago had turned into a philosophical discussion from an unlikely source. Who exactly was Andrew and how did he know so much about life and about people. The answer to that question would have to wait till next time while I focused completely on the task at hand.

The parking lot was almost completely empty by the time I finished the last flowerbed. I looked down as I was cleaning up and picking up all the supplies and the colors seemed brighter. Was it my imagination, was it the sunset or was it truly the fact that I had taken so much pride in my work that the flowers almost seemed grateful for what I had done and were rewarding me with brighter and more vibrant colors. I don't know what kinds of flowers they were but they were pretty. The bright yellows, deep purples and sharp reds blended together well and looked amazing. The sweet smell was strong yet not overwhelming.

I took everything to Andrew who was already heading toward the storeroom behind the building and locking up for the night.

"Good night my brother. Thank you for helping me today." He took my supplies as he flashed a broad smile.

"Thank you too. I'm the one who got the most help today. I'll be more aware of my labels and my thoughts."

He nodded and started whistling as he walked away. I watched him amble toward the front of the building and I realized that he was a man. A black man who had taught me so much in such a short time, not an uneducated gardener who before now, I would not have given a second thought.

Chapter 7 ~ Parental Discipline

It was getting dark when I left and I had to hurry home. Tomorrow was the first day of school and I had to get my books organized and packed before bedtime. I had been so involved with helping and learning from Andrew that I had forgotten to watch the time. The days were getting shorter as winter was approaching. I knew I should rush home to make it before dark but I was so busy thinking about what I had learned that I took my time enjoying the short walk home. Even the autumn breeze, which had turned cool this evening, did not bother me at all.

I knew I was in trouble when I walked into the house and heard everyone in the kitchen. Dad, mom and my brother were all at the kitchen table, the dirty plates in front of them indicating that they had already finished the evening meal. I overheard dad asking my brother if he knew where I was as I walked in and why I had not been home for supper. I say asking although it was more like screaming and interrogating.

Dad's approach to discipline was strict and based on fear. He was from the generation where fathers showed their love by setting high standards and doing whatever it took to make sure his children met those high standards. Corporal punishment was the norm for any infringement and compromise was not an option.

Discussion and arguing was unheard of and playing by the rules, his rules were the order of the day. These rules applied equally to both boys at all times. Love was shown with discipline and never shared verbally with the boys. Even birthday celebrations were trivial and a waste of time and money. It was only because of mom's insistence that birthdays were even celebrated at home and we boys were showered with gifts.

We knew they were from her even though she always put both their names on the cards and gifts.

Mom's approach to discipline was based on love and hugs. She would give you lots of love and expect good behavior in return. She would play the role of "good cop" against dad's high standards and "bad cop" approach.

"Your dad is expecting too much from you," she would tell us after we had been scolded then comfort us by lovingly lowering the standards that dad had set. She had a knack of modifying her approach to match each child's personality. In hindsight, she probably consorted with dad behind closed doors as they discussed how their parenting styles could complement each other as they disciplined us.

She also had a short temper at times especially after she had lovingly told you three times to do something. After the third request there would be yelling, screaming and throwing of whatever was close at hand toward any part of your body.

Hairbrushes, high heeled shoes and even plastic jars of lotion really hurt if you are not quick enough to get out the way. Mom also showed us love just as quickly and unexpectedly. Every few weeks she would decide to bake and decorate a cake or two on a Sunday afternoon. She would make a big production of this endeavor and she would always enlist the help of both her boys. Of course our way of helping was to play with the cake mixer and lick the blades clean when the frosting was done. She would smile and sing as we helped her and I treasured these bonding moments with her.

Dad's expectations were the same for everyone. He had no concept of personality styles and could not understand why my brother could build a birdhouse perfectly in an hour with no help or instructions while I would rather do a crossword puzzle than pick up a hammer. Dad was not much of a reader and my spending so much time at the library really upset him to no end.

I had left a note saying that I was leaving for the library which he had obviously not seen since he laid into me as soon as he saw me walk in.

"Do you know what time it is? We have already eaten and I've told you a hundred times that you have to be home for supper.

When hot food is being served you need to be here waiting for it not running around in the dark. You've missed supper and now you don't deserve to eat. Do you know what time it is? It's time to whip you into shape and maybe that will teach you to be home on time. Tomorrow it's back to school and your mother and I have been worried sick about you. Now you stroll in as if nothing is wrong."

"I'll speak to him, come here darling," I heard mom say as she rose from the table, took my hand and led me upstairs.

"Your father is just worried about you, you know? He just wants us to all eat together, that's all."

Sitting together in silence, afraid to have a second helping or being told that you were eating too loudly was really not my idea of a family meal. Not that I had anything else to compare it to really.

In my world the family meals on television were not realistic, just good acting when it showed a family sitting down together at the table, chatting, sharing and having fun while they shared the evening meal. At our table no speaking was allowed during the meal. Second helpings were met with a glare from dad or a scathing lecture on the evil of gluttony, how people in other parts of the world were starving and how fortunate we were to even have a hot meal. Reaching across the table was not allowed and you had to ask dad to hand you what you wanted, always preceded with a "dad may I?" and ending with a "please." Anything else and you got the lecture on rudeness and deserving a whipping to "beat some manners into you."

Everyone in the house, including mom I suspected, was afraid of the man and that was how he liked it. Nothing we did was ever good enough for him and he would destroy our self esteem by redoing what we had just done, right in front of us while explaining how we had screwed up and that his way was a better or easier way of doing it.

"Are you alright? You were at the library weren't you?"

"I'm fine mom. I just got wrapped up in what I was doing and forgot the time. I'm sorry. I'll pay more attention next time. It's just that…" I stopped mid sentence, debating on whether I should tell her about Andrew.

"It's just that, I like spending time at the library." I finished my sentence without telling her about my new friend.

I could feel her love for me as she looked at me and I knew that she would understand how important the library was for me.

She seemed to be the only one in the house who understood my struggles. Even with my bad grades, she would lovingly take me aside and tell me that she would always love me and be proud of me regardless of my grades.

"You'll get it," she would say, "I believe in you. I have faith in you, you'll get it."

After what I had learned from Andrew I realized that mom believed in me and would never give me a label of 'stupid' based on my grades. How I wished she could explain these concepts to dad and how much it would mean to his boys if he gave us an occasional word of encouragement.

Just one "good job" or "well done" instead of a lecture of "you know if you did it this way…." from him is what we all craved yet secretly knew that we would never hear from him.

"OK, get to bed. I'll go tell your father you said goodnight. You can read for a while and I'll come back in a little while to check on you. Remember, it's back to school tomorrow."

"I love you mom" came out of my mouth before I could stop it. Then I said it again "I love you mom" and truly meant it. She was a strong woman to maintain her sanity in this crazy family.

"I love you. I'll be back in a little while."

I don't remember her coming back into the room because I awoke to my alarm the next morning. Reaching over to hit the snooze button, I realized that I had not moved all night.

For the first time in a long time I had remained sound asleep all night, awoken refreshed and ready for the new school term.

Despite the scolding by dad last night I had slept all night. Could it be that I wasn't letting his label and his low expectations of me get me down?

Chapter 8 ~ Back to School

I arrived at school early, eager to get started with the new school term. I had been practicing my Xhosa with Andrew and couldn't wait to learn more of the language in class. Andrew had helped me take the language from the classroom to the real world. He would laugh at my pronunciation of certain words and teach me the colloquial use rather than the formal use that I was learning school. I appreciated how he made it a living language for me that I was forced to use when I was with him instead of simply memorizing vocabulary and grammar in the classroom.

When I arrived at school we were all ushered into the gym for assembly. I could feel the buzz of excitement as the students arrived, ready to put the events of the last few weeks behind us and start anew. We had only been gone for a few weeks yet it felt longer since I'd seen my friends. Not that I had many real friends anyway. Most of them were just classmates, except for Peter.

I had known him for six years and we often met after school and on weekends to hang out and have fun. This time though I had been so busy working and visiting Andrew that I didn't get a chance to see him while we were on break. I had not told him about Andrew yet and what I had been learning.

I smiled as I thought about addressing Peter with "Hello my brother" the way Andrew did whenever I went to see him. Peter saw me first and called my name as came over to me. He didn't give me a chance to speak because he started chatting right away about the importance of the new term. He wasn't exactly a studious person either so I was surprised about his excitement to be back in school.

We walked into the gym chatting about the weather and settled in for the customary first day assembly. We always started a new school term this way and the principal Mr. Petersen would spend at least an hour attempting to motivate the students with his usual boring speech that he did every few months. I had heard it so many times before that I could rattle it off if someone asked me to, including the same jokes. They were not that funny the first time he used them years ago yet they kept finding their way back into his well- memorized pep talk.

We would always oblige him though and laugh in the right places as if it were the first time we'd heard them. It was merely a formality before we faced the reality of the classroom and the term that lay ahead. Fortunately I would only have to do this one more time then I could say goodbye to my high school years forever and start my real life.

Not that I really knew what I wanted to do with my life. Mom and dad had been asking me for years if I knew what I wanted to study and I would always give them some made up answer. It ranged from attorney to teacher and of course doctor when my uncle was around but I had never seriously considered going to college.

During my junior and senior years I played the wishing game with family and friends and pretended that I really could become a doctor, dentist, teacher or lawyer – repeating the cliché that I could be anything that I wanted to be in life.

I had worked hard yet was unable to score high enough to enter the University that I wished to attend. Years of average grades ensured that I could not make the grade for University entry. I pretended that I was simply being lazy yet in reality I was struggling during tests even though I knew the subject matter.

Explanations did not matter though, only results. Dad could not understand how one of us could excel in accounting and not anatomy while his other son did the opposite. I managed to get through the subjects I was taking in high school with the minimal passing grade and saw no reason to continue the torture by going to college. Besides, there were two other factors to consider anyway.

The first was that my grades would probably not be good enough for college and secondly was the reality that I needed money to attend college. Mom and dad did a good job of not letting us know how poor we were by providing us with everything we needed, yet there were enough signs for me to see that we were simply surviving and they were living from cheque to cheque. They may not have had much money but they certainly had pride.

I was brought back to the present when Mr. Petersen cleared his throat and the old microphone crackled to life.

"Good morning students and faculty. Welcome back. I trust you all enjoyed your time off and you're ready to get back to learning. Please settle down so we can get started."

"Good morning sir," we all said in unison waiting for the formalities to be over and the pep talk to begin.

"The Easter break is behind us and it is time to buckle down and focus on your mid terms which will be here before you know it. I know that we all…." his voice trailed off.

Chapter 9 ~ Soldiers Again

A deep rumble shook the building interrupting his speech. We had heard that sound before and a hushed murmur spread across the gym. What were they doing here again? We weren't causing any trouble.

"Stay seated everyone, stay seated" I heard Mr. Petersen announce.

The scraping of boots on the wooden floor echoed across the gym as a line of soldiers in full riot gear entered and marched around the perimeter of the room and lined up from the stage to the back door. We were completely surrounded and trapped in the gym.

"Meneer (sir), Kom hier (come here)"

I heard the thick Afrikaner accent say from the back of the room as Mr. Petersen looked on from the stage. I knew I wasn't the only one who recognized that voice, a voice that caused fear in all of us. It was the unit captain, the same man who had led the soldiers during their raid on the school just a few short weeks ago.

"Stay seated everyone, stay seated," Mr. Petersen repeated as he left the stage and walked to the back of the room.

He didn't have to tell me twice.

I froze in my seat as the memories of my last encounter came flooding back. The memory of the first time in my life that I had stared down the business end of a rifle barrel and had felt the fear of impending death. The experience had helped cement my philosophical opposition to guns and weapons of any kind.

It was the one argument, the one point of contention and the one thing I disagreed about with my uncle. He loved all kinds of armory and weaponry and had a substantial collection at his house.

He had started collecting them during his days as a policeman and fell more in love with them when he spent time in the army. He often spoke about the power of having a gun and had a permit to carry a concealed weapon. He needed it for protection because of his stores he said.

He had offered to show me his collection many times and to teach me to shoot starting with the small caliber pistols and working up to rifles and shotguns but I had refused. Eventually we agreed to disagree on this point and respect each other's views.

He compromised by putting his jacket with his gun and holster in my parents' room when he came to visit on Sundays so I didn't have to see it.

Yet another reason I respected the man so much. How could he be dad's brother yet be so different?

A scraping sound brought me back to the present as the soldier closest to our row shifted position and his boots scraped the floor. He looked over to where I was sitting then shifted his gaze up again as he scanned the room.

I didn't move. I was afraid to breath too deeply in case the soldier standing a few meters away from me mistook my breathing as disobedience. I controlled my breathing, slowly looking around the room praying that everyone would obey and we wouldn't end up getting beaten and tear-gassed like the students I had seen on television.

"Look at that monkey in his monkey suit," a voice said from the floor. It was Peter. He had pretended to drop his pencil and was looking up at me from the floor as he spoke.

"Bloody monkeys, brainwashed and then given a loaded weapon. Monkeys following orders; that's all they are, monkeys following orders."

"Be quiet and get up, "I whispered reaching down to grab his shoulder and pull him into the chair. I looked up but the soldier closest to us was still looking away. Good, I thought he didn't see or hear us.

"Are you afraid?" Peter asked me as he sat up. He leaned in closer to me and continued, "You shouldn't be afraid of them, they are afraid of us. What they fear most is that we will start thinking for ourselves, not blindly following their orders anymore.

They fear that we are as smart or smarter than they are and that we will succeed in our mission to have a free, democratic country with equal rights for everyone. If you show fear they will keep you down my friend."

"Aren't you scared right now? I hear what you are saying but they are the ones in charge. Can we talk about this later when they leave? By the way, when did you become so politically savvy?"

"They will never leave. They may not be here physically with guns but the fear that they instill in us will never leave. A lot has happened since I last saw you and I've made some major decisions. Come over to my house after school and I'll tell you what's going on."

Peter's words reminded me of the lessons Andrew had been teaching me. In my heart I knew that they were both right.

Labels, I thought to myself.

Show them who is in charge and you will keep the status quo the way it currently is. It was easy saying I would not let labels influence my decision when I wasn't facing danger but could I do that when my life depended on it.

This is what Andrew had been trying to teach me and now Peter was reiterating the lesson. But this was a political cause and I was not politically inclined. I didn't want to die for a better education if I was already struggling in school.

I imagined that I was sweeping my mind clean but the fact that there was a soldier standing just a few metres away from me kept getting in the way.

Even if there were no law, we would still believe that we were meant to stay small. Andrew's words came back to me. Your labels will keep you in prison.

I felt a tug on my arm. Peter was saying something to me but I hadn't heard what he'd said. I looked over to him and was about to ask him to repeat it when the microphone came back to life.

"Let me have your attention everyone, let me have your attention." Mr. Petersen was back on the stage and the captain was standing next to him.

"The captain has informed me that there will be an army unit at our school starting today. They will remain with us indefinitely to protect us and help keep all of us safe while we learn.

If you need anything while school is in session please let your teacher know and they will let me know. Please remain seated while the captain and I have a meeting with the teachers. Teachers please come to my office right away. Students, thank you for your patience, you may speak quietly amongst yourselves but please remain seated. The soldiers will remain here until we get back. Captain, after you, right this way."

He followed the captain out of the gym as the teachers filed out and headed for the main office. I looked around the room as a low buzz started to fill the air and the students started whispering amongst each other.

I had a sinking feeling in my heart as I realized that my naïve notion of leaving the past behind and starting anew was not to be. The soldiers were not going away any time soon and the new school term was not going to be a new start for me.

This was the beginning of something big and I had no idea how far reaching this would be. I turned to speak to Peter but he was gone. I saw him huddled down in another row whispering to a group of seniors. They were all nodding in agreement and kept whispering amongst themselves when he moved away. As I watched him he moved to another group of seniors who leaned in to hear him speak. He had a serious look on his face and had them nodding in agreement to what he was saying.

I looked up at the soldiers around the room and was glad to see that they had not moved or made any attempt to silence the room. I guessed that as long as we were being fairly obedient they were simply there to maintain order in the room.

I smiled as I thought of Peter's description, monkeys following orders.

"Peter, what were you doing over there?" he had returned to his chair and was scribbling on the notebook he had pulled out of his backpack next to him.

"Peter, what's going on?" I asked again.

He looked over to me and put his arm on mine. "Look at me," he said in a very serious tone. "Our lives are about to change in a major way. This is going to be a senior year that we will never forget.

I know how naïve you are and how you feel about politics but I guarantee you that what we do now will be remembered for a long time."

"You're not going to do anything stupid are you? In case you haven't noticed, we *are* surrounded by soldiers with loaded weapons. Remember what happened a few weeks ago when they showed up? I've never been as scared as I was on that day and I have no intention of repeating that incident. I just want to get back to the books and graduate and the get the heck out of school. Is that too much too ask?"

"Yes and no" Peter answered slowly. "It's fine to want to move forward and finish school but you have no idea how big this is. Remember the stories we heard about Soweto and the other uprisings in the past? Each and every one of those people made decisions based on the benefit for the group as a whole not on what they would personally get out of it. They sacrificed their personal gain so everyone would benefit. After every incident there has been changes, it may not have been big changes but there were changes. This is big my friend and sacrifices are going to be made whether you like it or not. You will have to …"

He stopped mid sentence as the door opened and Mr. Petersen, the captain and all the teachers entered the room. The captain remained at the door as the teachers took their seats and Mr. Petersen returned to the stage.

"Quiet down everyone, quiet down. As you have all seen this term is starting off unlike any other. As I stated earlier, the captain has confirmed that his unit will be here every day to maintain order in our school. Starting tomorrow, all classes will be in session as usual. When the bell rings for you to move classes please do so quickly, quietly and efficiently. There will be armed soldiers around the school everyday including the entrance. You may not leave the school premises during lunch break or use the playground. Stay in your class during lunch and move quickly between the classrooms. After school, leave the premises immediately and go straight home.

If you have any questions you may ask your teachers during classroom time tomorrow.

I am sending you all home right now and we will resume tomorrow.

The teachers have offered to start calling your parents today and informing them of the situation.

Please gather your belongings and start leaving from the back row. Do not gather in groups, speak to each other or loiter on the premises.

Go straight home and come back tomorrow morning ready for a great day of learning. We'll see you all tomorrow."

The soldiers and the captain stepped aside as we all arose and started to exit the building from the back of the room. It was eerily quiet as we each silently waited our turn to leave. My mind flashed back to the last time I had faced the soldiers with their weapons pointed at us.

Although there were no weapons pointed at us this time I felt the same fear in my heart. I felt helpless and subservient.

Armed soldiers had ruined my first day back at school and I felt helpless, yet angry that they had the power to do so. I was following orders, just like the soldiers and had no say in the matter. The more this thought took hold, the angrier I became at how quickly things had gone awry this morning.

Chapter 10 ~ Political Rumbling

"My house in one hour, O.K. one hour," I heard Peter say to someone behind me. "You too, "he tapped me on my shoulder, "my house in one hour, it's very important."

"O.K.," I muttered as my row started to move.

I walked toward the gate of the school and looked up to see a white van pull up and park outside the front gate of the school. It was the local news crew and I watched as a cameraman and a reporter with a microphone in her hand got out of the van.

News had spread that the military had surrounded our school and they were here for the story. I kept walking and headed home deep in thought. Mr. Petersen had made a wise decision, dismissing us early instead of letting the incident become a story on the evening news.

It seemed like the weight of the world had come down on my shoulders. My school, my school in my town was becoming one of the schools that I had seen on television where the political action was taking place. It was no longer a picture on the tube, it was real and I had no idea what to do or how to handle it.

When this had happened at the schools on television things never ended well. The students would taunt the authorities with their political ideals and the military would show up in riot gear with teargas and rubber bullets to quell the unrest and restore peace. Of course in the process many students would be arrested, injured or even killed.

There were new rules in place since the political fervor had begun where the police and the military had the right to arrest anyone, of any age, that they suspected as instigators and hold them indefinitely as political prisoners without notifying the parents.

Many students were still missing around the country, presumed to be in custody while their parents tried to get verification of their whereabouts. Now the situation had arrived in my town and at my school. A state of emergency and a curfew on students would soon follow like it had in other cities.

I walked home quickly and instinctively turned on the television as soon I was in the living room. I flipped through all three channels over and over again, not really sure what I was expecting to see. The daily soap operas were on and there was no mention of anything else. Not even a breaking-news alert about the army at my school. Just like the last time, I thought. I had faced death a few weeks ago and it had not been important enough to make it on the news back then either.

I decided to take Peter up on his offer to meet at his house. He was older and wiser and perhaps he could shed some light on the situation. I opened the door and checked the street for military vehicles. I was relieved to see a quiet street though I'm not sure what else I was expecting.

"Boo!" my brother startled me as he came around the corner of the house "isn't it cool that we get the day off today? An extra day to play, an extra day to play," he sang as he entered the house oblivious to the seriousness of the situation.

"I'm heading to Peter's house, see you in a while. Make sure you stay home O.K.?" I called after him, "did you hear me?"

"Yeah, whatever. Hey wait; can I have your sandwich? O.K. bye," he answered from the kitchen with his mouth full from the sandwich he had pulled out of my backpack.

The route to Peter's house went past the school and I debated for a moment on whether I wanted go a different way that would add an extra ten minutes to my walk. I decided against the alternate route and walked past the school. The army and the news crew had left and the parking lot was mostly empty. It seemed that most of the teachers had left soon after we did.

A few houses away from Peter's residence, I was surprised to see many cars parked along both sides of the road and his driveway full as I walked up to his front door. I could hear many voices as I opened the front door and walked into a packed house.

The living room was filled with most of the seniors and there were teachers present as well. The kitchen table had an assortment of snacks and drinks laid out with paper plates and plastic cups neatly stacked at the end of the table. The people entering would help themselves to snacks then filter into the living room to chat in groups.

Some groups were standing around, others chatted while seated on every available surface including folding chairs and lawn chairs that had been brought in to the room.

"Thank you for coming everyone, Thank you for coming," I heard Peter say. "Did you all get something to eat? If not, go grab something now so we can start the meeting."

I walked over to him as he was directing people into the packed living room while calling out to someone to go find more chairs.

"Peter, hey Peter. What meeting? Why are all these people here?

"Find a seat, you'll know in a few minutes when we get started."
I did what I was told and found a place to stand behind the couch.

I was standing next my Xhosa teacher and it felt strange to see him out of the classroom. I didn't even know that he knew Peter or how on earth he would know where he lived. I had many more questions yet did not get a chance to ask them before Peter started addressing the crowd.

"My brothers and sisters in the struggle. We have a decision to make today, a decision that we knew we would have to make someday. We have been meeting for weeks now, well not all of us" he looked directly at me then at a few other people in the room, "and the time has come to take a stand."

"We must take a stand to support our brothers and sisters around the country because we no longer have a choice. We can no longer deny that change is in the air. We can no longer watch the action on television and not get involved because we think we are not being affected. We are affected and we are oppressed. It's time to accept the truth my brothers and sisters, time to stand up and be heard. It's time for solidarity. People are dying for the cause. People are being arrested. People are speaking out.

The world is watching; it's now or never. What are we going to do to contribute to the cause, our cause, to gain our independence?"

"Amandla! (Power)", someone in the room called out "Awethu (to the people)" the room replied in unison. This was the rallying call that had become common during the struggle.

People would chant this affirmation with a unified voice, right fist pumping the air as they marched into 'battle' against the oppressors around the country. This chant kept them moving forward…moving forward towards the police and the army in riot gear, moving forward to severe beatings and rubber bullets and indefinite arrest. Moving forward to gain freedom from the oppressive regime of the white man in power. This was a chant that was foreign to a naïve student like me who had stayed away from politics all his life and was not about to get swept into the fervor of rallying with the crowd.

I suppressed the urge to run away and secretly feared that this loud chanting would alert the army who may be driving by. They would undoubtedly storm the house and arrest us all. How would I explain that to my parents I wondered?

Peter continued with his political message. "We must join our brothers and sisters around the country. Join in the boycott of our inferior educational system. This boycott is specifically for the seniors – we are the leaders of our school and we must show the country that we are one with them. I know we have discussed this over and over again and now it's decision time. Who's with me on the boycott? Who is with me? We have representatives here from all four of the senior classes. Teachers, Thank you for joining us as well. Raise your right hand if you agree with our plan of action."

I looked around the room as the hands came up in agreement from the senior representatives. A few of the teachers who were present raised their hands as well to show their support of the decision. The students and teachers of my school, my school in my insignificant little town had now joined the ranks of hundreds of schools around the country in staging a school boycotts by the seniors.

I was seeing a political coup in action and I was scared as I realized the magnitude of what was happening. My comfortable secure world was crumbling and I was confused about what to do. Do I stand with my fellow students and join the boycott or do I retreat back into my cocoon?

This was a life changing decision that would affect my future and I was afraid of what it may bring. I left Peter's house with visions of being arrested and jailed or beaten and tortured as a political dissident. As I approached the library on the way home I wondered if Andrew was there this early on a Monday morning. I decided to go see if he was available to perhaps guide me as he had with his previous life lessons.

Andrew was nowhere in sight as I scanned the garden area and the side of the building. I walked around outside and did not see him working anywhere outside. The weather was getting colder and I knew he wouldn't be doing much outside work on these colder days.

Entering the library I asked the lady at the reference desk if she had seen him and she nodded.

"I think he's still upstairs" she replied as she pointed the way.

Chapter 11 ~ Mindset

I ran upstairs, two steps at a time and found him unpacking books from a big box onto a cart for the librarian to mark and categorize. As expected he was totally focused on what he was doing and doing it with love. He would bend down, remove a book from the box and dust it off carefully. Then he would look at the front and back cover before placing it on the cart.

I wondered how many of the titles he could actually read as he was dusting them off.

"Andrew, I just have a few questions for you, it won't take long," I blurted out without even saying hello.

"There will always be questions my brother and after you get the answers you will have even more questions. That is the beauty of life. The good news is that all the answers to any question you have are inside of you. There will be very few that you cannot answer once you learn to listen and to tap into the amazing power that is inside of you, inside of all of us. Remember to remove the labels from your mind. What can I do for you my brother and why are you not in school right now?"

"I need your help. Something huge is happening and I'm not sure what to do. The army came to the school again today and we dismissed early."

"Take a deep breath. Slow down and start over. The army came to your school today?"

"Yes. Did you see the army roll in this morning? I have to discuss the serious situation that is happening at school."

"Yes I did. Were you there when that happened? I wondered about that and would like to hear more about it. I can see how scared you are and I'm sure you are confused too.

You have many questions don't you? You are safe in here for now. Help me with these books, take a few deep breaths and tell me what answers you seek."

"Fine. Let's get these books unpacked quickly so you can answer my questions. OK?"

"I've already started answering your questions you just haven't heard me because you do not yet realize which questions you need to ask."

"Would you please stop with the mumbo jumbo and give me some advice. This is serious and I need your help." I was getting frustrated and angry. I was still in fear of the soldiers and anxious that I had been present at a meeting where a political group had made a radical move. I needed to make a decision and I didn't know whom else I could turn to for advice.

"Anger and fear, yes I know them well. I am not intentionally making you angry or avoiding answering you. Anger is fine as long as you let it show then you let it go. Holding on to anger will only hurt you especially if it is something that you feel is out of your control. Control is something we all want yet is the wrong thing to strive for. The only control you have is over how you respond to the stimulus. You have choices – you always have a choice. The only one who can truly help you is you. This is a process that anyone can and every one should learn. Only you can help yourself and how you respond is a choice. Come help me unpack these books and I'll explain further. Is that alright with you?"

"Yes, of course. I'll calm down while I help you and ask questions while we work," I answered as I reached down to take a book out of the box. I relaxed and became more aware of my breathing. His voice comforted me and I felt confident that he could help me make sense of it all.

I casually wiped the front and back covers as I was looking at him, placed it on the cart and reached into the box again.

"Yes, please explain" I repeated. He smiled and reached for the book that I had just placed on the cart and handed it back to me.

"Excellent. Let's start with this book. The answer you seek is right here in this book."

Surprised by his answer I looked at the cover wondering how he knew that this particular book would help me.

"Caring for your tropical fish," I read out loud, "what does that have to do with my questions. I was going to ask you about what is happening right now. I'm scared and I have a tough decision to make that will affect my future. Are you saying I need a fish tank to calm me down? "

I looked up from the book in my hand as I heard him roar with laughter. He was laughing so loud, slapping his knee in the process that he didn't even notice all the patrons staring at us. His loud guffaws and bent over posture had broken the golden rule of silence to be observed in the library and there was no doubt in my mind that everyone in the building could hear him.

I had never heard him laugh before and the sound of his laughter made me start giggling and temporarily forget my troubles. The librarian was walking over to him to tell him to be quiet so silence could be restored.

He tried to stop when she came over to him "So sorry miss" he said between giggles "I didn't know my brother was so funny, so sorry." He tried to stifle himself but it made him start laughing again.

The few other patrons present on a Monday morning were quietly giggling like I was, trying to contain themselves as the contagious nature of his laughter echoed through the library.

It was quite a sight seeing the expression on their faces as they watched this big, black man uncontrollably laughing and not knowing what was so funny.

Even the librarian had a smile on her face.

"OK you two," she said in a fake stern voice.

"Take it outside for a few minutes and come back when you can control yourself. Andrew, we need to get these books done. All right everyone, back to what you were doing, "she announced to the onlookers as she gently pushed Andrew and me to the staircase and gave me wink.

"Get him to calm down before he comes back in here."

"Come on Andrew." I pulled my giggling friend down the stairs and out of the building.

"What was so funny anyway? You told me that that book would help me and I need an explanation."

Andrew had finally calmed down and put his arm around my shoulder as he answered me.

"Not that specific book," he said "the job that we were doing. You see, you want to rush so you can get to what you think is important instead of focusing on what you are doing. Just like the flowers, my brother. You should not casually dust it off and put it away. You need to appreciate the book for the power that it holds. It took the author many hours of thought, many hours of writing and much time, effort and frustration I'm sure to get that book done. Now we are blessed with it and need to show it much respect as we place it on the shelf and it fulfills its purpose. You and I will never know how many lives that particular book and every other book in there will change as they read it."

Andrew's voice had grown serious as he continued.

"We can only know that the book will somehow affect the reader and we have to respect it for the power it holds. Just like you did with the flowers last time. If you can respect a flower or a book for the power it holds, you will be able to respect yourself and other people too. Respect leads to love, even if it is only one way in the beginning. There are no labels when there is respect and love."

"Yes, about those labels…" I started to say as I realized that his wisdom was building on the previous lessons.

He interrupted me before I could finish and continued with his message, "You pick up a broom and people see you as a janitor, not as a person any more. People see the broom and automatically assign a label to what they see and therefore react a certain way."

"Yes, I know. So how do you stop people from doing that? That is my main question for you Andrew. I have been more aware of my labels and not judging people for what they do but for who they are. Yet, I'm finding that I am still being treated the same way. How do I stop people from treating me badly?"

"You cannot change the way other people see you until and unless they are ready to change. What you can do is stop reacting to their expectations. In your head and in your heart you must know, truly know that nothing and no one can affect you.

You have a choice about how you respond. Whatever comes your way is simply a way of making you stronger not an intentional act of sabotage against you. Our labels say we must fear the police and the army with their guns and their uniforms. They are people too, simply doing the job that they are paid to do."

"Wait a minute. What about the police and all the tension that is taking place across the country? The police can stop anyone from succeeding."

"Do you really think so?"

"Well, yeah, the police are showing their force by arresting people and stopping them from moving ahead. I think that it's OK to be scared of them."

"Enough to let them keep treating you like an animal because of the colour of your skin?"

Was Andrew going to start a political discussion I wondered as I answered him? "I don't think that's their fault, they are just upholding the law."

"You've made two important points but you have confused the two. The first point is that you must respect others. Whether it is the police or the janitor, you must respect your fellow human beings regardless of who they are, what they do and even how they treat you. It doesn't matter if they are black or white; they are still your brothers and sisters. Respect must be earned not forced by fear."
He paused for a moment as I nodded and listened.

"The second point is that thinking gets in the way of action. If you know that you can move forward in life no matter what comes your way, your actions automatically move you forward and no thinking is needed. Our brothers and sisters in the struggle are not thinking about themselves. In fact they are not thinking at all. Not about the obstacles and the problems that they must face. They simply know what must be done and they do it to achieve a successful outcome. Success will come when you have the right mind no matter what the situation looks like right now."

"Andrew, what you are describing is Mindset. Are you saying that it is your mindset not your surroundings or your circumstances that determine your outcome? Hold that thought, let's go back inside I have an idea."

I ran into the building and pulled two dictionaries off the shelf to look up the definition of mindset. Andrew had followed me inside and was walking toward me as I looked up from the second search in the dictionary.

"Here it is. '*Mindset – The set of beliefs that you will move forward no matter what comes your way.*' This one says '*Mindset - A fixed mental attitude or disposition that predetermines a person's responses to and interpretations of situations.*' So your mindset is the basis for success no matter what you do."

"Yes, I like that" Andrew said nodding in agreement "Mindset. You mindset shields you from fear if you are taking the right action. It doesn't matter what other people think of you or how they act toward you if you have the right mindset. It's tough to argue and talk yourself out of something when you have a positive mindset. You will know who you are instead of believing the label that others give you."

"Mindset Determines Outcome. That's what you are saying aren't you Andrew? The only option is to keep your mind open living moment to moment as you move toward your desired outcome." My mind was rolling and I kept going with this new and exciting concept and awareness.

"These moments occur every day if your awareness is open to it. Most people live in their closed worlds and have no idea this is occurring and how powerfully their lives can be positively changed every day. During those rare moments when it does cause a flutter in the tightly knit fabric of their lives, they question it endlessly then dismiss it as coincidence or imagination. If only they knew that their expectations of failure had caused them to fail, not their surroundings or their circumstances. I think that…"

"Stop thinking." Andrew was shaking me. "Stop thinking and start doing. Let's continue this discussion upstairs. We have more books to unpack."

I followed him upstairs, my mind in turmoil over this new concept. How could I apply it to my life with all the craziness that was happening at home and at school these days? I tried to quiet my mind as I focused on what I was doing.

I followed Andrew's lead, showing each book the respect it deserved as I dusted off the covers and placed it on the cart. Andrew asked me to push the full cart to the librarian while he went to start on something else.

"Here you go miss. Your books are ready."

"Thank you young man. I've seen you helping Andrew a few times now as he does his work. I was beginning to wonder if you had been hired and I was supposed to be paying you. Are you a friend?"

"No, I haven't been hired to work here" I smiled and continued, "I guess you could call me friend although he is more like a mentor than a friend. He has helped me in many ways; he is a very smart man."

"Really, you think he's a smart man? He's been helping you? I know he does good work and always seems to enjoy himself. I'm not really sure why but he's always smiling no matter what he's doing. A little strange if you ask me. No one can be happy all the time."

I smiled and started to walk away. Yes you can, I thought to myself, with a positive mindset you can.

She smiled back at me and turned to go back to her desk as I walked back upstairs to go learn more from Andrew.

Mindset Determines Outcome, especially since having a positive mindset requires no thinking and no judgment. Mindset is responsible for the person to work their way out of an oppressed society yet is also responsible, if not done completely, for that same person feeling unworthy and depressed.

Andrew had his head inside the huge box that we had just unpacked when I returned. He was removing the wood that reinforced the bottom when I saw him.

"O.K., I understand the concept and how much your Mindset Determines Outcome. Now how do I apply it to what is happening at school? As a senior I'm almost expected to boycott school and stand with them but I'm not sure I want to do that. I have to think about the consequences of my actions and how it will affect my future. I've never had to make such a huge decision before."

"Come over here," Andrew said as he gestured for me to come closer. "I hear people talk about thinking outside the box and that is why they are taking a stand against the regime. Let me show you something. Get in." He pointed to the huge empty box.

"Get in, what do mean get in? Into the box?"

"Yes, get in and kneel down." He pulled me closer to the box. I got in and knelt down, curious to hear his explanation.

"Do you see all the information available to you?" he asked as he pointed to all the books around the room.

"All the information is here, all the answers, if you know where to look. You are blinded when you remain in your box," he explained as he closed me into the box.

"When you are in your box, your world, all you see is what you know even if you don't like what you see. Then you are told to think outside the box and it confuses you. How can you think of something, especially a solution to an issue, when your current environment – your box, restricts you? It's like me asking you to see the world through my eyes, through the eyes of a black man. It is not possible."

"OK, so how do I get out of my box?"

"You don't. You acknowledge that your box exists and accept that it has limitations and therefore the solution cannot be found in your current reality. Get out of the box and I'll show you a solution."

I stepped out of the box and stood to the side as Andrew picked up the four pieces of wood that reinforced the base. He moved the box out of the way and placed the four pieces of wood on the floor in the aisle between the shelves in the shape of a square.

"Now step inside the square," he said. Change the word box to Frame. Your frame is your world. The great thing about a frame is that it is not as restrictive as a box and it can be expanded. You learn and grow by Expanding Your Mental Frame.

When you realize how important your, what did you call it mindset is for success, you can convert your solid box into a frame. Now as you expand your mental frame you'll find the answers that you are looking for. Look how close the solution may be."

He was pointing to the wood in front of the bookshelves as he continued his explanation.

"You may only need to expand a little bit and you'll reach a whole shelf of answers. Acknowledge that your box or frame exists and that it is limiting your progress then expand your mental frame to find the answers."

"Wow! I get it. I have to work on expanding my mental frame. Great, now how do I do that?"

"Be careful my brother, be careful. It's good to be excited when you understand a new concept. The excitement does not last long though when you step out into the real world and realize that the rest of the world has not changed and will seem to be working against you. It's very easy to be sucked back into your box because you are comfortable there. You may not be happy but you are comfortable. When you have applied this new concept and you have seen results then you can be happy.

"Knowing what to do and actually doing it are two totally different things. People know that they should exercise to be healthy yet they do not do it. People know that they should work on their relationship with their wives and children yet they do not do it. People know that you should respect everyone regardless of race or religion yet they do not do it. Instead they make Apartheid a law so they can blame the law and feel better when they do the wrong thing. Blaming someone else, blaming the government or blaming the law, shifts responsibility away from you and makes you feel helpless. Doesn't it feel better for my white brothers and sisters to treat me like an animal, a laborer and servant instead of a person because the law says they have to? Equality will come at a high price if the law ever gets changed. If my people ever get the power over the whites their frame will dictate that they oppress them in the same way in order to feel justified and compensated. I hear everyone speak about equality and civil rights for all races. How about human rights regardless of race or religion or anything else? How about connecting and respecting each other as humans?

Your frame can take you out of here when you expand it and it will keep you shackled when you don't.

People are walking around with their frames so ingrained that it has become a mental prison and there is no escape. I'll say it again; *I would rather be physically oppressed than mentally suppressed.*

At least we can blame the law for our stupid, idiotic actions. Will a school boycott change the law? That is the question you should ask yourself.

Situations and circumstances do not make you who you are, they reveal who you are. More specifically, it reveals who you are within your current frame. Are you taking an action to stand with your brothers regardless of the result or are you taking an action because it is the right thing to do? Unfortunately or maybe fortunately for you, you also have to listen to your parents.

Decisions should be made with the power of a positive mindset and an expanded mental frame. This taps into your inborn dynamic ability to move toward opportunity without thinking and without regard to current circumstance. "

"Let me think about that for a while. I need to process how expanding my mental frame will help me decide what to do. How will I know if I've made the right decision?"

"Eish! My brother," he exclaimed and walked over to slap my head. "You will never make the right decision if you think about it. Expanding your mental frame requires feeling, not thinking. Thinking gets in the way of tapping into your subconscious mind and holds you back. Remember what we said earlier, how could you think about something that is outside of your current reality? You have to feel it. Spend some quiet time and listen for what comes up. If you can make it through all the noise, then the feelings will come through from your subconscious mind and guide you.

"Listen without thinking, without judging and you'll get the answers you seek. People have so much mental noise, so many judgmental thoughts based on their old frame throughout the day that it's hard to get clarity. They close their eyes and after what seems like an hour they open their eyes again and realize that only two minutes have passed. Society teaches us to be dependent, to look for solutions on the outside instead of trusting ourselves. Expanding your mental frame helps you create the mindset, the intuition, to trust yourself."

"O.K. I'll let that process for a while without thinking about it." I glanced at the clock as I left the library and was surprised to see that it was almost four already.

I had to get home before mom and dad did, there was much to discuss tonight. As I walked home my mind kept swirling between two images.

The first was of me being trapped in a box, frantically screaming for help and clawing around in the dark then it would jump to an animated portrait. I was looking at my face on the wall surrounded by a wooden frame. My eyes would shift left and right looking at the frame surrounding me then I would start smiling as my hands emerged from out of sight, reach through the wall and start expanding the frame.

Chapter 12 ~ Taking a Stand

I was surprised to see both cars in the driveway when I arrived home and wondered why they were home early. This question would soon be answered as I entered the house.

Mom, dad and my brother were seated in the living room with the television on. I walked in just in time to see the video footage on the news report of the army surrounding our school. They cut to an interview with Mr. Petersen explaining why the army was at the school today and that they would return daily to protect the students. I could tell by his strained voice and limited body movements that he was following a carefully rehearsed script. I could see the tension in his face and imagined the captain standing next to him waiting to jump in if he said the wrong thing or tried to add to the message.

Dad looked up as I walked in and told me to sit down. After the newscast he turned off the television and cleared his throat as he thought about what to say. Mom shifted nervously in her chair.

"This is quite a situation we have here, isn't it?" he said as if still in deep thought then looked up at me then at my brother then back at me.

"I received phone calls from Mr. Petersen and some of your teachers explaining what had transpired at school today and why you were sent home early. I want to know from each of you what happened today. Your mom managed to get out of work early to come home and you were not here," he said glaring at me.

"Your brother said you had gone to Peter's house, is that correct? Tell your mom and I what happened today? You go first, and then tell us why you felt the need to leave here instead of staying home to look after your brother."

I was looking down at my feet but I could feel dad's eyes on me as he waited for me to answer him. I avoided looking at him and looked at mom instead while I thought about how much to say about the day I had.

Mom smiled as her gaze met mine and she nodded slightly as if to say "its O.K. you'll get it." I could feel her love and see the concern in her face, yet that simple phrase that she endlessly repeated to me-you'll get it-gave me the courage to gather my thoughts and tell my parents the whole story.

I knew I had to expand my mental frame and share everything with them or risk getting stuck inside my own box. Andrew's words came to mind just before I spoke, 'I would rather be physically oppressed than mentally suppressed'. Unleash the mental shackles that are holding you back to create a positive mindset.

"Mom, dad" I said, controlling my voice and holding back the emotions that I had felt today.

"As you now know, the army surrounded the school today and marched into the gym during assembly today. What you may not know is that today was the second time that they were there. They came a few weeks ago, just before the holidays to break up the groups of students who were singing outside the school. Apparently they have been watching the school for some time and they say there are a lot of politically active people at school."

"The second time?" mom and dad asked in unison.
Dad continued, "Are you involved in this political mess? I've told you before that if you want to get involved in this mess it's your own doing. I'm not coming to get you out of jail if you get arrested. Why don't you just behave and stay out of trouble. These troublemakers are going to get themselves killed. Is that what you want? Your mom is worried about you and how you've been acting lately. Look at her. Are you trying to keep her awake at night worried about what you are up to? Were you part of this political rally last time?"

"It wasn't a political rally; we were just singing songs to show our support. It seemed like no big deal at the time and we weren't doing anything wrong. Do you realize how many students are getting arrested and all we are asking for are equal rights."

I was surprised at the emotion in my voice and how much I was saying, almost arguing with dad. I was coming out of my shell and letting my voice be heard because my opinion mattered.

"We, did you say we? So you are involved in this mess?" Dad was struggling to keep his voice and his temper under control. He was looking at me over his spectacles and breathing deeply, the classic indication that he was upset and about to blow.

"You know we love you, don't you?" Mom spoke, obviously stepping in to give dad a chance to cool down, "we are concerned about your safety and about the disruption that this may bring. You are a senior and we want you to finish up without any trouble at school."

She had come over to me and was holding my hand as she continued speaking. "It's hard for me to believe that what I was seeing on television all this time is now happening right here. I suppose it was inevitable and even though it bothered me it is now affecting me directly and putting my sons in danger. I'm sure you were scared and confused today. Are you getting involved in politics at school?"

I could feel myself relax as she spoke and appealed to me with love and logic. She was so different from dad in her approach. Empowering me to make a decision and saying she trusted me rather than being the dictator that dad was. I avoided answering her direct question about my involvement.

"What else do we need to know about?" dad asked from across the room, still fuming.

"The seniors have decided to stand in solidarity with the other students around the country and boycott for right now. From what we have seen and heard, the police or the army will keep students inside the school property and stop them from having meetings and rallies but will not come after those who are boycotting and staying home unless you are on the streets or around the school property. The world is watching, sanctions are being imposed and the world is calling for Mr. Mandela to be freed and for equal rights in this country. I don't know what will happen or how long it will take but I must do my part. Mom and dad, you can give me your input and your advice but I feel that I must make the decision for myself and right now I haven't decided if I'm in or out.

I am with everyone in spirit though I must still decide on my actions. What I do know for sure is that I do not want to be around soldiers with loaded automatic weapons who seem to be waiting for the order to fire. I have looked in their eyes and I did not like what I saw."

It was the closest I had ever come to being disobedient and it felt great. Not that being disobedient felt great, being able to voice my opinion, expand my mental frame and stand for something without being rude or disrespectful even though it may go against my parents felt great.

There was a palpable tension in the room. Mom was grinning; she had a wide, proud grin across her face. My brother was at the edge of his seat looking at each of us, his mouth slightly open with surprise at my audacity to speak to my parents in this way.

Dad had sat back in his chair and was now leaning forward again preparing to speak.

"I was going to say that you are wasting your life but it sounds like you've made up your mind. I forbid you to be part of this mess and I will not support you if you get involved. What do you think mom?"

"I think he will let us know what he wants to do. I may not agree with him but I have to love and support him in his decision. We have always taught the boys to think for themselves and to follow their heart. It sounds like he's not taking this lightly or following blindly and I have to respect him for that. I'm proud of you," she said looking directly at me.

"I'll wait for your answer. In the meantime, what about the rest of this week, are you going to school or staying home? If you choose not to go to school, will you at least promise me that you'll stay here and not go outside at all?"

"I'm going to school tomorrow," my brother spoke for the first time. I don't understand all this stuff and I'm staying out of trouble. I'll be in school tomorrow."

"Yes mom, I promise" I looked over at dad waiting for his response. He smiled at mom and scowled at me but did not say anything else. He got up slowly and left the room without saying another word. A few minutes later I heard his bedroom door close and the muffled sounds of the television coming from the room.

"O.K. then, it looks like the family meeting is over. What would you like for supper? She asked nonchalantly and walked into the kitchen. Come on boys; come help me get supper going."

We helped mom get the cooking done and set the table. Mom went up to tell dad that supper was ready but he never joined us. We ate in silence and mom took a plate of food into the bedroom for dad.

It was my turn to do the dishes and I gladly accepted. It gave me time to ponder my new mindset and how I had stated my opinion and taken a stand. I was not being rude or disrespectful; I simply wanted to be heard. Wasn't that the whole point of the political changes occurring in the country, the need to be heard and treated fairly and equally? By the time I had finished doing the dishes everyone had retired to their rooms. I passed my parents bedroom and heard them having a muffled, hushed discussion, about me I presumed.

I got up at the regular school time and helped my brother get ready for school. Dad was still not speaking to me and merely grunted when I attempted to converse with him. I had to admire him though for at least saying goodbye to everyone, including me when he left for work rather than just leaving the house. I secretly again longed for a "good job" or an "I love you" from him but I knew it would never come.

Mom obliged with a hug, an "I love you" and a stern warning to keep my promise and stay home when she left for work.

It was strange being home alone on a school day. I had not realized until now how eerily quiet the house was with everyone gone. The silence was freaky and I turned on the television for noise. That was boring so I popped a movie into the video machine. A movie may help me escape my current reality in the action scenes like reading did.

It didn't work very well since the shooting scenes reminded me of my close call with the soldiers and got my adrenaline pumping again as I recalled the burning eyes of the soldiers. The squeaking sound of the VHS rewinding sounded loud in the quiet house. I was taking a stand by staying home, yet I wished I were in school. At least in school I was being productive and on my way to graduating. Was I doing the right thing?

I was questioning my motives. Is this what having a positive mindset feels like? My thoughts were interrupted by the ringing telephone echoing through the house.

"Hello"

"Hi mom. I'm fine. No, I haven't decided yet if I'm going back to school tomorrow. Yes, I'm staying inside the house. Yes, I'll vacuum. O.K., I'll see you tonight. Love you too."

I hung up with her and sat back on the couch. I was glad she called to see how I was doing. Maybe I should speak to her about what I had been learning from Andrew and see if she could understand my dilemma and help me clear my mind. I don't know, maybe?

My decision was to stay home today and I got my way. A minor victory for a teenager, but how would that affect me in the future. Maybe dad was right; I shouldn't get involved in politics.

I had been happy in my world. No, I wasn't, I was ignorant to what was happening around me. Denial, that's it, I was in denial and pretending to be happy.

Clean your mind my brother, sweep your mind of the negative thoughts and expand your mental frame. Andrew's advice came to me. It wasn't simply a thought; it was a deep, penetrating voice that interrupted my chaotic mind like watching a movie with the volume turned up.

I saw myself sweeping the walkway at the library and felt the emotions of being ignored as I did on that first day. My subconscious mind was replaying the experience and I was reliving it completely. You're sliding back, my brother I heard Andrew say, keep sweeping. Acknowledge that your mind needs cleaning or you'll stay stuck.

A vision of Andrew's face appeared on the white wall surrounded by a picture frame. He grinned widely and his eyes widened as his hands came through the wall, grabbed the sides of the frame and started pulling it apart. Expand your mental frame, my brother. "It is always necessary, yet never easy my brother." I heard him say as he faded away and I became aware of my present surroundings again.

I had walked into the kitchen and was holding a broom in my hand. I started sweeping the kitchen floor, and then moved to other areas of the house. Then I pulled out the vacuum cleaner.

I was floating around the room not bogged down by negativity, actually enjoying the task of vacuuming which I typically saw as a chore. I had become an automatic cleaning machine. Dusting came next and the furniture polish came out after that.

I realized the wisdom of Andrew's philosophy and couldn't help laughing as I was cleaning the bathroom. I was intentionally focusing on my cleaning and doing it with love and respect for myself and for my family – my whole family. It felt good to do something without expecting a reward and it gave me time to process what was on my mind, even while scrubbing toilets.

Negative thoughts would come through while I was focusing on a cleaning task and I would simply let them bubble from the depths of my subconscious mind without judgment. The less I thought, the quicker they would dissipate. Then feelings would come through and beg for judgment from my conscious mind that I couldn't give because I wasn't focused on it. The negative feelings would hang around for a few minutes while then get weaker and weaker before fading away. It was interesting to observe how the positive feelings did the exact opposite. They would get stronger and stronger and give me a jolt of energy, then would settle into my body with a warm, tingling sensation. It was like watching a magic show on stage and knowing the outcome before the illusion was revealed. I was experiencing Andrew's philosophy of no thinking and no judgment in action.

I was under the kitchen sink putting the cleaning supplies away when I felt the hair on the back of neck rise. I pulled the cap off the furniture polish and with my finger on the trigger slowly backed out and turned around to see if anyone was there.

"Boo!" my brother said from the kitchen table.

"You must be really bored if you've been cleaning so much, looks good though. You should stay home a few more days and clean my room tomorrow."

"You scared the pants off of me," I said reaching down for the cap and putting the furniture polish away. "I didn't realize what time it was."

85

I had been cleaning for hours yet it seemed like minutes. Time had stood still and I was amazed at how much pride I took in doing the work when I did it Andrew's way. I understood why he was always smiling even while doing what I had always considered menial tasks. So this is what expanding my mental frame was all about.

The next few days were pretty much the same and passed quickly with dad ignoring me most of the time. Mom would call after she got to work and then again in the afternoon to check on me. I debated many times whether to ask for her advice during her afternoon call since I was still questioning whether I was staying home for the right reason.

The telephone rang on Thursday afternoon when mom called to check in. Before she said goodbye she asked me to get something specific out of the freezer to thaw for supper.

The reason for the specific request became clear when she said that my uncle would be joining us for supper tonight. Baked Snoek was his favorite meal.

By the time I came downstairs again after a long, hot shower and tidying up my room, mom was just coming home.

"Perfect timing" she said when she saw me. "Go get your brother and we can get supper started."

I found my brother in his room, reading his science textbook and doing some projects from the back of the book.

What a nerd, I thought to myself, just a few days into the new school term and he was already reading ahead and doing the projects.

"What are you doing?" I asked snidely.
"Just doing some reading to see what's ahead," he replied matter-of-factly. "We should get to this chapter by next week and I'll already know how to do some of it."

I was about to make some sarcastic remark but stopped myself as he continued speaking, "it's good to plan ahead, "he finished.

"Mom's home. She needs us to come help her with supper. Let's go. We need to wash our hands and get down there."

"Just a minute," he answered with his head in the book again. "Let me just make a note here to read this section again, it's a little confusing. O.K., I'm done, let's go."

Labels, my brother, I heard Andrew's voice again as we walked to the kitchen together. Learn from him instead of labeling him or you'll get stuck again.

"Can I ask you a question?" I muttered humbly.

"Sure."

"Why are you reading ahead? Why not wait till you learn it in class?"

"I don't know. You probably think I'm a nerd like everyone else does but I don't care. I just like to be prepared for what's coming."

"Not anymore. I apologize for thinking that way and I respect you for what you do. You've always done that and you've always been an A-student. I should learn more from you instead of just seeing you as my baby brother."

"Cool. Thanks. So if you are liking me more now, can I use your bike on Saturday?"

I smiled and admired him even more. He had accepted my apology and my compliment without question or doubt. I should learn to do that too. I would decline compliments and find a reason why I did not deserve the accolades. My life would be so much easier if I simply said thank you and moved on.

"I wouldn't go that far," I answered, "you are still my baby brother you know." I lifted his arms over his head and was tickling him when we entered the kitchen where mom had already started preparing the food. She had changed her clothes and had all the ingredients laid out on the counter but had not started cooking yet.

"Come on over chef" she said to me as we entered and took my hand. "You are cooking tonight."

Mom had been teaching me to cook for a while but had not let me prepare a full meal before. How ironic I thought to myself. I had been expanding my mental frame all day and now I could continue by being in charge of the evening meal.

"O.K., start the rice first since it takes the longest. Do you remember what to do?" I nodded and proceeded.

Under her watchful eye, I prepared the rest of the meal with only minimal help from her. My brother was in charge of handing me the seasonings as I asked for them.

"How was your day today?" she asked as I was putting the seasoned fish into the oven.

"Not as weird as the first few days, I kept busy."

"I see all the cleaning that you've done since you've been home. Thank you for doing such a great job. I don't think I've ever seen the furniture shine that much. I've been begging you for a while to help with the cleaning, and then you surprise me by doing such a great job. I knew if I kept hounding you, you would get it." I smiled and nodded. If only you realized how much I had learned over the past few days, I thought to myself. If only you knew.

"Yes, mom. I get it. I'd like to discuss something with you before dad gets home."

"I hope its quick then. He'll be here soon and your uncle is coming tonight too."

"Yes, it's quick. Why is he coming to visit tonight anyway?"
"He didn't say. Maybe he knew we'd be having one of his favorites tonight. He loves this meal and your dad does too. They are definitely brothers."

"No, I get along with my uncle. Dad isn't like him," I replied sarcastically.

"Yes he is, more than you know. You need to give him a chance to see you as an adult. He still sees you as the little boy who had trouble learning to ride a bike and who slept with a nightlight till you were eight. He's just being protective and he does love you even though he doesn't say it. He believes in showing love more than saying it and the fact that he let you get away with what you did last night and today is a sign of progress."

"That's what I want to speak to about, before dad gets home. I've made a decision." The answer had come to me while I was in the shower. I started to dismiss it then remembered all I had learned and waited for the feelings to follow. I watched the process unfold in my mind and the end result, my decision on what to do, felt right. I wanted to share it with mom first, partially so I could practice what to say before letting everyone know.

Chapter 13 ~ Major Decision

"What have you decided?" Mom asked and brought me back to the present.

"I've decided to stand with my fellow students and join the boycott. I have been going over the pros and cons all day and I have a final decision. You and dad may not agree with me but I feel like this is the right thing to do." I held my breath and waited for her response.

I had no idea how she would react with such a big decision. As far as I could remember, this was the first time I was standing up for myself and making a life-altering decision without input from my parents.

"Are you sure about this? It's your senior year and you are blowing your chances of graduating. Nobody knows how long this mess is going to last. What are you going to do all day, stay home and clean every day? I know this is not something that you decided quickly without looking at all sides. Gee whiz, you drive me crazy with how much research you do before you make a decision.

Remember how we had to go to ten different stores to find the bike you wanted because of all the research you had to do first? When are you going to tell your father?"

Mom was right. I would do an endless amount of research before making a final decision whether it was for my bicycle or my clothes and was one reason I loved the library so much. Today I had not thought about what to do. I had used Andrew's method of "no thinking, feel it" to decide what to do. I was calm and confident in my final decision.

"Yes, I'm sure. I'm letting everyone know after supper tonight depending on when our guest leaves. How long is he staying?"

She didn't have a chance to answer because we heard the garage door open and the doorbell ring at the same time. Dad and uncle must have arrived at the same time and he was ringing the doorbell while dad came in through the garage.

My uncle was a prankster and would rather see us confused by the ringing doorbell than come in with dad through the garage. Oh well, we loved him anyway and my brother went for the front door while I went into the kitchen to check the fish.

"Is that delicious aroma what I think it is?" I heard him say as he came into the house, "did you make rice with it too?"

"Thank you dear," he said as he gave mom a big hug, "your wife knows how to spoil me on a Thursday evening," he said to dad who was just walking in.

"Don't thank me, thank your nephew," she said looking at me as my brother and I were setting the table.

He winked at me then walked over to my brother. "Thank you my boy. I didn't know you could cook," he said smiling as he picked up my brother and threw him over his shoulder before swinging him around the room.

"Stop goofing around, supper is ready," I announced in a pretend stern voice.

We sat down and enjoyed our meal. It felt like a family meal on television because my uncle kept joking around and teasing throughout supper. It was so different from what I was used to and it seemed that my uncle went out of his way to do the exact opposite of what dad was doing. He kept chatting and repeating his questions until dad would answer. He would get up, walk around the table and pick up what he needed instead of asking dad to pass it to him. My favorite part was when he would see that my brother's or my plate were half full and he would dish more food into it with much fanfare and say "eat up young man, you're a growing boy."

I looked over at dad many times to see him just shaking his head and attempting to eat in silence but failing because my uncle kept hounding him to engage in conversation.

Mom was having a good time too and matched my uncle's sarcasm at every turn.

After the meal, we were asked to clear the table and start doing the dishes while the adults started conversing at the table.

I volunteered to wash and he could dry and put the dishes away. I preferred washing rather than the two-part task of drying first then putting them away. Mom had taught us this chore early on and made sure that we understood the process of washing. Start with cups and glasses first, then silverware and bowls. Plates go into the water last and pots and pans require extra dish soap to cut through the grease and soak for a while before cleaning. Dry and pack away as you go so you don't have a counter full of dishes when you are done. Oh and never dry the inside of a glass or cup with a dishtowel because it leaves lint on the inside of the glass.

My brother had carried all the dishes into the kitchen and I had just started filling the sink when mom called us back to the table. They wanted us to be part of the discussion they were having. My uncle started first, explaining how quickly the unrest was growing.

More schools around the country were holding political rallies and the police, in full riot gear, were showing up to quell the resistance. He had made some calls to his army contacts after he saw my school on television and wanted us to know what he had learned. The army would be at my school and patrolling the area for the next few months. They were carefully watching certain students and teachers at my school who were known to lead political activities in the past. He turned to me and surprised me by asking me the question that I dreaded, in front of my parents.

"You are in a tough position and you have a choice to make. Are you going to join your fellow students and teachers in the school boycott or are you going to cross the line and stay in school? My sources tell me that they are not expecting many seniors, as well as some teachers to cross the line and they are on high alert to quell any issues right away. Their orders are pretty much to shoot first and ask questions later. What are you going to do?"

My breathing became shallow and my heart raced as he finished the question and turned to me for an answer. I glanced over at dad who was biting his bottom lip and looking at me over his glasses – the classic 'you're in trouble' look as he waited for my reply.

The other two at the table were holding their breath and looking at me and at dad. I'm sure they were wondering if he was going to erupt immediately or wait until I answered the question before going into his typical rant that we all knew so well.

I took a deep breath as I formulated my answer and fought the urge to run away without answering at all. Perhaps I could use the distraction technique of answering with another question so he would be forced to answer, giving me more time.

I purposely looked up and met dad's angry gaze directly, holding it until he looked away first. Then I looked over at mom who was slowly nodding her head before looking at my uncle to answer.

"Well," I said stalling, "it is a tough choice. You've made it even more difficult now that you've told us that it will not be ending soon. Any idea how or when this is going to end?"

"I only know what I've already told you. As you know, the world is watching us and the unrest is getting worse. The violence and the boycotts are now hitting almost all the Black, Coloured and Indian schools around the country and affecting all of us. When it was confined to the townships it was easier to deal with. I hate to say this but there will be many more deaths before this is over.

I have a feeling that it will take some significant changes politically, not just a bigger army presence to make this go away. More and more people are joining the struggle, ready to give their lives for a better South Africa. This has been brewing for many years but it feels different this time. I've never seen any political issue spread as fast or involve as many people as this one is doing. Something is going to happen, no, something *has* to happen soon or this will not end well.

This reminds me of what happened to Rosa Parks. One person's action sparked a nation and started a movement in America that had many deaths and many victories as well. That was thirty years ago and very far from our shores but its impact was felt around the world. I don't know how this will end in South Africa but I pray that thirty years from now we can look back at this time in history and say that it led us to a better place and had an impact on the world.

We can no longer ignore what is happening and pretend that we can carry on as we always have. You see how it's affecting you and I'm sure you know that the decisions you make now will impact the rest of your life. What are you going to do?"

"What do you think I should do?" I asked.

"You are going to do the right thing and do as you are told. You need to get back to school and behave yourself." Dad had been waiting for the right moment to take control. "There is no choice in this matter for you. You *will* do as you are told."

"Hold on a minute," my uncle chimed in while I was being scolded, "give the boy a chance to speak. We know what you want him to do; I'm asking him what he wants to do."

"He has no choice," dad reiterated, "Political decisions are for adults not for children. Children should be seen, not heard and he is a child."

My uncle scowled. "Are you serious? He is a senior in high school and he needs to make his own decision. You cannot live his life for him and you cannot make him do anything."

"Yes, I can. While he is under my roof he does what I say he does. He is just a child and he shouldn't make decisions about things he knows nothing about. That's it, end of discussion."

"That's it, end of discussion. That's how you are going to end this conversation?" my uncle asked with an irritated tone of voice. He was getting angry but had not raised his voice, yet.

"It's not your problem. This is a family matter which we'll finish later after you leave." Dad was taking charge of the conversation again and shutting it down so he could be in control. I wondered to myself with whom he would discuss it later since he never involved mom in discussions. He was the man of the house and he made the rules.

I looked over to my uncle who was in deep thought about how to respond. I could see on his face how hurt he was about dad's comment on it being a family matter.

"So you saying I'm not family, is that it? Tell me then, oh wise one, how many political issues have you been involved in? I can respect your point about family but I want to know how *you* can decide on something that you know nothing about either. It's not like you…."

"Stop it, both of you." Mom interrupted and we all turned to look at her in surprise as she continued "you two are arguing and you haven't given any one else a chance to speak. Have you asked me what I think about this? Even more importantly, have you asked your son what he wants to do? You have no idea what he's been going through or how much this whole thing is bothering him. You refuse to acknowledge what is happening and how serious it is."

Mom raised her voice slightly as she continued. "This is one situation that you cannot ignore and hope it goes away quietly because you have spoken. Yes, you are the man of the house and you make the decisions, I know, to protect us but this is different. We just went through this a few days ago and he's been home all week. Why don't we ask him what he wants to do and listen, truly listen to what he has to say? Would you at least give us that much?"

Dad nodded without saying a word and looked at me while avoiding eye contact with mom. I could tell he was angry and I momentarily debated whether I should back down and do what I knew he wanted or follow my heart and tell him what I had told mom earlier. The image of me being trapped in a box in the library came to mind and I felt stifled and helpless as I formulated what to say. In my mind I was about to scream for help when the top of the box opened and Andrew's hand came in to help me out of the box. He smiled and led me to the frame and started expanding the sides without saying a word. His silent, smiling face told me what I had to do. I looked over at mom then at my uncle. He was at the edge of his seat with his elbows on the table and his head in his hands looking directly at me, waiting for my reply.

If it were not for the vision of Andrew and the lessons he had taught me, I would have backed down and submitted to dad.

I couldn't do that now. This time was different, this was the new me. I was surprised at how calm I was, how unafraid and how sure of what I was about to say. I looked over at dad.

Before I could speak, in my mind I saw an imaginary frame surrounded his head, tightly squeezing his face. Then bars appeared from the top to bottom of the frame with a loud metallic clunk as they appeared from left to right across the front of his face.

He was trapped in a mental prison unaware of how stuck he was in his frame. I had a choice to make, feel sorry for him or stand up for what I believed.

"My decision," I said slowly "is not an easy one. It has been bothering me all week as I've watched things get worse at all the schools. Now after hearing and seeing the response of the army and knowing that a political shift that will inevitably happen I feel like I have made the right decision. *I have decided to stand with my fellow students and join the boycott.*"

Dad let out a deep sigh. I heard my uncle gag in surprise and my brother say a quiet "whoa!" under his breath. I looked over at mom who sat silently, almost in shock that I had actually followed through with my decision. She waited for dad to respond. Dad took a moment for my words to sink in and shifted in his seat. I was half expecting him to jump out of his chair, reach across the table and grab me to 'shake some sense into me' and tell me how stupid and childish my decision was. It didn't happen.

I relaxed for a moment and felt an inner pride for being brave and applying the lessons I had learned from Andrew. Everything from mindset to clear your mind had culminated in this life changing decision that I could utter to the man that I feared most in life.

"What do you think of what your son has said?" he asked mom. The way he phrased the question told us that he was angry yet holding back. Whenever my brother or I were in trouble we were labeled as 'your son' or 'your children' to mom and when we did something he approved of it was 'the boys' or 'the children'.

"Well," she said looking at me "it sounds like he has made his decision. I know it wasn't easy for him but I also know that if this is what he has decided then he must feel strongly about it and I have to say that I will support him in what he wants to do.

Whether I agree or disagree is not relevant. This is his life and his decision and I will love him anyway. It's not like he's doing this to go against us or to get out of school …are you?" she asked as she looked in my direction. I was shaking my head from side to side and mouthing 'no' so she continued and looked back at dad. "He knows the consequences and he has made a tough decision. That's all I have to say about it."

"So what's next for you then? Are you going out and being part of the rallies and activities out there? I've told you before if you get arrested because of this nonsense it's your fault. What if you get killed? Am I supposed to stand over your dead body and say I told you so or am I supposed to cry for you because you were supporting your fellow students? What are you going to do all day long, sit around here and do nothing? You've already cleaned the whole house over the last few days."

Dad had a point. I had not thought about what I would do all day although I had definitely decided not to go to any rallies or political events. I had seen the emotions rise when I was at Peter's house. I had been around political activists and seen and felt their passion before. I applauded their willingness to stand up and be seen but I knew that I was not one of them. I would do my part and not go to school but I would not go out and taunt the enemy, I mean the army. Having looked into the eyes of both a political activist and a soldier I chose not to be part of either one's world.

There were only two people who could help me decide what to do, Mom and Andrew. I would have to sneak out of the house tomorrow to go see Andrew and ask mom for her opinion after work tomorrow night before dad came home.

My internal dialog was disrupted as my uncle spoke up, "he can take on some hours at the store. He did well when he was working during the break and I can certainly use a good man to help out. I'll send him to the second store with his cousin and we can arrange a pickup time for the morning. He'll be out of the house and away from here during school hours and I'll check on him all day to make sure he's working hard. What do you think?

Brilliant, I thought to myself. I would rather stay busy and be out of the house, away from the television and away from the school while making money as well. I waited to hear what mom and dad thought of his idea. Dad spoke first "you don't mind getting him rides back and forth to work and keeping him busy?" he asked.

"Not at all, it's what I would and in fact am doing with my son right now. That's one of the reasons I came over tonight, to find out what he was doing about the boycott since my guy decided to join in as well. We had a similar discussion with him last night.

He'll be joining me at the main store so I can teach him the business. What do you think; is it a go then?"

"Fine with me" dad answered quickly. It was almost as if he were glad that there was such an easy solution and I would be under the watchful eye of my uncle.

"Tomorrow is Friday, you have one more day at home then off to work you go on Saturday. Is that OK with you two?" Both my mom and my uncle nodded in agreement. Dad got up from the table and walked into the kitchen with a deep sigh and not another word.

"Anyone for desert?" mom asked, releasing the tension in the room and changing the subject. We still seemed to be on edge and everyone visibly relaxed after mom spoke.

"Hey doc, any new magic tricks to show me?" my uncle enquired, also attempting to help change the subject.

I was glad he asked because I could answer in the affirmative and it gave me a reason to get up and go to my room.

"Yes, I'll go get the new illusions from my room. It's called an illusion, not a trick you know?" I was relaxing as well and excused myself as I went to my room.

When I returned, dad was nowhere in sight and mom had moved everyone to the living room. I had been practicing some new card tricks and did them with much flair and mystery. He was most impressed with the water in the newspaper illusion though. In this illusion the magician unfolds a newspaper and pages through paper showing the audience that there is nothing hidden inside. The newspaper is then folded in quarters and water is poured into the top. While the water is being poured, there is no sign of it leaking through the pages. The magician pages through the newspaper again, with no sign of the water present.

After uttering the magic words, he unfolds a corner and magically returns the water to the glass.

My audience applauded loudly with a "how'd you do that?" coming from my brother and my uncle. It felt good to have everyone 'enjoying' themselves together without the tense energy that dad brought into a room.

My uncle left soon afterward, after going upstairs for a little while which I presumed was to speak to dad who must have been upstairs. Mom came in to say goodnight and gave me an "I'm proud of you, I knew you'd get it" quick pep talk before she left.

I felt exhilarated, yet exhausted and I must have fallen asleep quickly and didn't remember much after mom left the room.

I awoke from a pleasant dream and looked over at my clock. I felt refreshed and was wide awake a full ten minutes before my alarm was set to go off. I knew this feeling. It was the same feeling I'd had before when I had developed a positive mindset and cleared my mind of labels. I also felt a sense of accomplishment after having taken a stand for something I believed in and letting the world or in this case my parents know about it. I was proud of myself and I knew mom was too. I had to tell Andrew how I had applied the sequence of steps he had taught me to make a tough decision. I had to go today since I would be at the store all day tomorrow. I lay back down on top of the covers and stared at the ceiling mindlessly, truly mindlessly with no thoughts at all. This is what a clear, no thinking mind felt like.

I heard the commotion in the rest of the house and was surprised to hear the garage door open as I got in to the shower. I came down and saw that my brother was still eating breakfast and mom was getting his lunch ready.

"Where's dad?" I asked looking around.

"I guess he left early." mom replied in a puzzled voice.

"I didn't think he had any early meetings today but he's gone. He didn't even take his coffee with him."

"I know it's my fault isn't it? I took a stand for what I believe in and now he's mad at me."

"Ok, I'm outta here. Bye mom, love you. You can clean my room today Ok?" my brother taunted as he left for school.

"Sit down for a minute. Listen, I meant what I said last night. You are almost an adult and *you* have to make the decisions that will affect your life. I know you didn't make this lightly and I respect you for what you want to do. Legally you are an adult when you turn eighteen, yet 24 hours prior to that you are still considered a child. How does a birthday suddenly make you an adult? It doesn't and I think that's part of the problem in society.

We treat our children like children, shielding them from the tough decisions and the negatives in life until midnight on their seventeenth birthday then BAM! They are adults the next day and we open the floodgates of reality on them. No wonder they make silly decisions, they screw up and they fail because they were never taught to be adults. You are sixteen and you've made an adult decision that could potentially affect the rest of your life. I am truly proud of you. I love you and so does your father, don't you ever doubt that. He just shows it in a different way. OK, I'm off to work. Do you need anything before I go?"

"Thank you mom. I appreciate what you've said and it does make me feel better. I do need a favour though and I wouldn't be asking if it weren't important. May I leave the house for a little while today? I have to go see a friend and I'll come right back. Just to one place then back home."

She smiled at my last statement before she answered. "As your mother, I do not recommend that you go out of the house. You heard what your uncle said last night. On the other hand, as your mother who is seeing you become an adult, I have to trust you when you say it's important. So I'll leave it up to you to decide. As long as you are home when I call this afternoon. Starting supper before I get home has really been helpful too."

She kissed my forehead and walked out of the house without waiting for me to reply. I watched her drive off then came back into the kitchen to mull over what she had said. I was excited to hear her comments knowing that she had sincerely meant what she said.

Mom was not one to mince words; she let you know what she thought when she thought it. There were many times when she had scolded one or both of us in public. It did not matter whether we were in the store, the street or even in our friend's house.

I now realized that she was simply being her loving, caring self showing us her love not purposely embarrassing us in front of our friend or for the benefit of the many strangers who had witnessed this phenomenon over the years.

Back in the kitchen I noticed that everyone had taken full advantage of being home once again and not even cleared the kitchen table. Putting away the cereal made me realize that I had time for more than a quick bite since I was not rushing off to school.

The library did not open for a little while and I took advantage of the time by making a hot, cooked to order breakfast for myself. Nobody else in the house liked my vegetable combination in omelets so I treated myself to a fluffy 3-egg vegetable omelet with extra cheese and toast. Two cups of coffee later and after reading everything within reach including the ingredients and the labels of all the breakfast items, I washed the dishes and headed to the library.

I was nervous being out on the street on a school day again but I made it to the library without seeing an army patrol. I walked past the backpacks strewn along the outside wall and realized that library time was part of the school day for some of the younger children. The library was busy for this time of the day and I wondered if it were always this busy on schooldays.

All the people at the desks were helping the patrons so I walked around looking for Andrew. I took advantage of knowing my way around thanks to Andrew and snuck into some backrooms that he had shown me, usually off limits to the patrons. He was nowhere in sight so I exited through the side employee door.

I checked the gardens even though I knew it was getting too late in the season to do any gardening. As I walked toward the storage room I saw a ladder against the side of the building. I stepped back away from the building and looked up on the roof to see if he was up there.

"Andrew, are you up there? Andrew!" I called.
"Good morning my brother," I heard him before I saw him. He must have been in the middle of the roof because it took a few seconds before I saw him peek over.

"Happy Friday to you. I'll be down in a few minutes, OK?" he said then disappeared again before I could answer.

I paced impatiently waiting for him then felt guilty because I was intruding on his work time. I hoped I wasn't getting him in trouble by showing up so often and speaking to him. I'm sure he couldn't afford to lose his job and I would feel really bad if he did because of me.

He descended a few minutes later. "Sorry to bother you Andrew. I'm not going to get you fired am I? I know I've been here a lot lately and I appreciate all the lessons."

"You worry too much, my brother. You've been helping me and I appreciate what you've done for me too. Thank you. What can I do for you today?"

"How have I helped you? I'm the one who needs to be thanking you for all that you've taught me. I won't take up much of your time today. In fact, I'm here to let you know that I've decided to join the boycott and stay out of school with the other seniors. My uncle has offered to let me work full time at the store and I don't know when I'll have time to come see you again. So, thank you again."

Andrew put his arm around me. "Mindset. You taught me that word the other day and how it describes in one word what I was explaining. It has been a pleasure meeting someone of your age who is willing to open their mind and shift their mindset. Is this your final decision or are you still thinking about it?"

"No sir, there was no thinking. It felt right and there was no judgment or labels involved, just like you've taught me."

"Well done my brother. A decision made without thinking. It sounds like you have chosen to wake up my brother. You know that moment upon awakening when you are not quite awake and yet not asleep either? That zone when you can choose to either wake up completely or fall back asleep? Most people are in this zone, not really knowing whether they are awake or asleep in life and merely existing through the daily grind oblivious to the world around them. They are working toward an unknown something, whatever that mysterious something may be for them without really living. Well it no longer applies to you. Choose to wake up, my brother. Give yourself permission to fully awaken to life and to admire the wonders around you.

I hear people say that the sky is the limit. I disagree. Right now, at this very moment in time our lives are changing and we are standing for something. Right now my brother, the sky is not the limit, the sky is the floor. The only limitation is the one that we put on ourselves. Get out of the way and enjoy the ride. It will not be an easy ride, waking up really is hard to do, though it will be worth it in the end.

Stop your whining and choose to live every day as if it were your last day on earth. Congratulations on waking up and have fun in the working world."

"Wow! Another powerful lesson and it's the one I needed to hear right now. You have answered my question before I even asked it. I shall continue waking up thanks to you. Good bye my friend."

"Hamba Kakushle (Go well) my brother."

I will miss him I thought to myself as I walked home. My decision is made and I'm ready for the working world. I'm on my way to adulthood and it was pretty easy. Why did the adults make it seem so hard when this is all it takes? I was feeling very grown up when I arrived home. I pulled out the vacuum cleaner for my last day of cleaning before being a full time worker. I did my cleaning duties in silence as I contemplated how much Andrew's lessons had influenced me so far and how these concepts could apply to any area in my life. I had already seen some of them in action with my parents and had used his non-thinking method to take a stand and join the school boycotts. His last words were still on my mind: The sky is not the limit the sky is the floor.

I was dancing around the living room with the vacuum cleaner when the phone rang. It startled me and I tripped over the vacuum cleaner and chair just as I was moon walking across the living room. With my legs still tangled in the cord I reached for the phone,

"Hello. Hi mom."
"No, I'm fine," I answered when she asked why I was panting.

"I'm fine," I repeated without further explanation "vacuuming right now."

Mom gave me a few instructions for the day and I hung up. I stayed on the floor for a few minutes rubbing my back while laughing at my silliness and how great it was to see the new me taking shape. Despite the pain and muscle spasm in my hip and back I felt wonderful.

I was setting the table when everyone got home and we ate supper in silence. Dad didn't say much except for reminding me that my uncle or my cousin would be picking me up early for work. Mom advised that I get to bed early since I would be working all day. I happily obliged.

Chapter 14 ~ The Working World

There was a knock on the door early the next morning when my uncle came to pick me up. He said hello to everyone who was getting ready to leave and waited as I finished my tea before going out to his van. I was his first stop as he picked up employees in the townships on the way to the store.

"Are you ready for your first day as a full time employee? How do you think you will do at the second store?" he asked as we drove off.

"I think it will be fine. The question is what you think since you are the boss. Please be totally honest with me about how I do. I do not want special treatment because I'm family. I am there to do a good job and work to your standards" I replied.

"I'm serious. I want to know how you think I'll do. I know you have high standards and I want to earn your respect and earn the position I have without any leniency because I'm family."

"I appreciate you saying that. I have watched you and you seem to be doing well. In fact I'm going to give you a little more responsibility while I have you here until you decide if or when you are you going back to school. I know you haven't decided yet so it's not a big deal when you say you are ready to leave. My guy hasn't decided about school yet either and he'll be doing some business training with me right now. I'm even going to open on Sundays for a little while because people are asking it. That means that you get to go to the other store with your cousin and help him run that one for now."

"My goal is to have the boys each running one of the stores by themselves pretty soon. That way I can grow the third one, hire a good manager for it and think about slowing down a bit.

Retire is not a word in my vocabulary but I'd like to do some travelling once I know they feel comfortable running things without me. Would you do that for me? Would you help out your cousin by running that store with him, I would really appreciate it? "

This was an unexpected turn of events for me. I had not really considered that he would send me to another store. I knew he trusted me and probably saw this as way to give me a hands-on business experience while I wasn't in school. Personally I would have preferred if it were with him since I didn't get along with his son. Surely he knew that we didn't get along yet he was still asking me to do this for him and I trusted his business instincts. Reluctantly, I agreed.

"I'll do it for you since you asked and I'll do my best to make it work. Thank you for this great opportunity, I think."

"Thank you. You can spend the day with me and I'll have him come by here to take you home tonight. He'll pick you up tomorrow around the same time I did today. Thanks again."

Weekends are really busy and the store filled quickly. It didn't take long before I was running around serving customers and the steady flow of customers had me on my feet all day. Even the lunch break seemed like a blur and I was on the floor again pretty quickly. I felt like a different person as I gave each customer my complete focus and attention.

My cousin drove me home after work, his bizarre choice of music blaring loudly so he didn't have to speak to me. We both knew that there was no love lost between us and he would intentionally do things that he knew would upset me. For example, he wouldn't even pull into the driveway when he dropped me at home. He stopped in the street in front of the house with the car still running and his music on while I got out.

Without even looking at me or saying goodbye he peeled away as soon as I shut the door.

Mom greeted me excitedly wanting to know how my first day had been while she prepped for the evening meal. I told her it was fine and told her about my uncle's request.

"Is that alright with you?" she asked, "I know the two of you don't really get along."

"I'll be fine. Do you need help with supper?" I assured her and changed the subject quickly. I was hoping it would be fine but I didn't need her worrying about me any more than she already did.

I realized how tired and sore I was during the meal. It was the first time I had really sat down all day and I was falling asleep at the table. So this is what a full time job felt like? Now I knew why mom and dad were always so tired at the end of the day.

I excused myself to my room. I fell asleep quickly and awoke to mom's voice. Mom came in to make sure I was awake what seemed like minutes later but it was morning already. I was stiff and sore but ignored the pain, hoping a hot shower would help ease the discomfort, as I got ready for work. I was now a 'full timer' and I wasn't going to complain about some minor aches from my silly clumsiness with the vacuum cleaner.

Chapter 15 ~ Life in the Working World

I had not even started breakfast yet when I heard the horn of a car blast three times. I looked out and saw that it was my cousin, parked in the street trying to get my attention. I said goodbye to everyone and walked out. He was earlier than expected and I was embarrassed by his rudeness. It was early in the morning yet he showed no respect for the neighbors as he sat in his car with his music blaring and his car shaking from the loud speakers. As expected, he peeled away with his tires squealing as soon as I shut the door without a glance or a greeting.

This was going to be a long day spent with my least favorite person. He had to pick up a few workers on the way and I enjoyed seeing the happy expressions on their faces when they got into the car and saw me. Speaking loud enough for me to hear above the music, all three shook my hand and said it was good to see me. I had never worked with them but knew them from visiting the store over the years and I knew how loyal they were to my uncle by working for him for so long.

After we had unlocked the store my cousin called a brief staff meeting. He explained that we would both be at the store for the next few weeks then barked out orders to each of us and walked off. While we were all getting the store ready, I saw him go make some tea for himself and put his feet up on the desk in his father's office with the morning newspaper while we all worked.

After the first customer walked in he put the newspaper away and turned on the charm.

He knew that his father had a good reputation in the community and my cousin's superficial charms fooled the customers into thinking he was as kind as his father. As the day progressed I literally gagged a few times as I overheard the lies he told customers. I minded my own business and did my work.

Weeks went by and nothing changed in the store. I had not told anyone about his fake sincerity and had hoped that he would change his behavior. The more I worked with him, the more I disliked him and that feeling was unsettling. My aching back even seemed to get worse when I was around him. He treated me like a second-class citizen at the store the way he had always done and it was even worse when it came to the other employees.

At any point in time regardless of whether the store was busy or others were present he would reprimand someone for even minor issues right away. He found some perverse joy in being able to literally shame someone into submission. Respect was a one-way street and he freely exercised his power and wrath on every person who worked for him regardless of age, experience, responsibility or job title. There were many days when I walked away feeling powerless as I watched him exert his power. Ironically, he actually had no idea about how biased and prejudiced he was toward those who had less than him, including family members like me. He thought he was the "cool boss".

He would sit down with us – his lowly workers – and join the conversation like was one of us. I did not have the heart to tell him how much they despised him. He was perceived as pretentious, arrogant and out of touch with reality by most of the employees. Of course as the only family member working for him I was expected to pick up the slack. In his mind he was doing me a favor by giving me the great privilege of working with him. It was implied that my job was safe because I was family.

Unfortunately the rest of the staff was not that lucky. No person was immune to his wrath, including employees who had worked for his father for many years. I felt the shame and embarrassment as I watched him disrespectfully yell at Sam, an elderly gentleman. Even though Sam worked slowly, he always managed to finish all his tasks at the end of the day. I could relate.

I worked slowly too whenever I could now that my back was hurting more and more. Sam was a hard worker and a loyal employee who had been with the company for many years. In fact, Sam had helped babysit my cousin when my uncle opened this store years ago.

I was confused about what to do. On the one hand I knew I should be thankful for having a job and to stop dreaming about this magical life that I had created in my mind. My current circumstances and lack of funds were my destiny in life. On the other hand I was doing this for my uncle not my cousin and a constant feeling of settling-for-less kept me awake at night. I had to let my uncle know about his son's behavior and hope that he believed me. He had trusted me enough to send me here and I had to let him know.

My cousin must have sensed that something was on my mind as I was constantly watching him while he managed the store. It was almost lunchtime on a Wednesday afternoon when he approached me.

"Do you have any plans for lunch today?" he asked, sounding like he really cared.

It was actually a silly question on his part. He had seen me have lunch for weeks now. I brought a sandwich from home and ate in the storeroom or outside enjoying the last of the sunny Autumn days. I would make tea in the break room or occasionally splurge and buy a drink from the store and flip through the local paper until I returned to the floor. Lunchtime varied as we all took turns to eat between customers. My cousin, 'the boss', was the only one who could take a break at any time.

"Plans? If you call what I usually do plans, then yes I have plans. I plan to have my sandwich in the storeroom today." I answered sarcastically. He was not one for friendly banter with anyone especially me so I brushed off his question with sarcasm.

"Good, so you have no plans then. I'm taking you to lunch today, my treat. When I picked you up this morning I saw that a new restaurant on the main road by your house is now open. We'll go there today. Does that good? Give me about thirty minutes then we can leave, OK?" He walked off before I could answer leaving me wondering why he was buying me lunch.

Dining out was a luxury that I was not used to.

My parents had done a good job giving us all we needed and hiding the fact that we did not have much money. As I got older I realized how hard they worked and how little was left at the end of the month. Mom would kindly and lovingly dissuade and talk me out of extra curricular activities over the years. Initially I thought it was out of concern for my wellbeing until I realized that the real reason was lack of money. Eventually I stopped asking to do anything that required payment. As I looked back on my uncle's frequent visits on Sundays I was sure he was lending dad money when he needed it.

"OK, let's go." I heard my cousin say as he came over to where I was stocking shelves. He turned to one the employees, "hold down the fort, we'll be back in a little while. Thanks pal, I owe you one," he winked and gave him a high five then turned back to me, "I'm hungry, let's go. I can't wait to try out the new place. Have you been there yet? Probably not, I know they just opened the other day."

He continued conversing all the way to restaurant while I simply nodded and listened to him ramble on. I knew it had to be something serious if he was actually speaking to me, not listening to his music. I kept waiting to hear why he was taking me to lunch but he avoided the subject while we were in the car.

As we entered the restaurant, he turned on the charm and flirted with the hostess and the waitress. I'm sure he believed that his wit and sarcasm was being well received. We ordered our meal and he turned his attention to me.

After some small talk about the décor of the restaurant he said it was time for a serious discussion. He started off by telling me how well his life was going and how proud both him and his father were of the job I was doing. I was well liked by all the regulars and I had received numerous compliments and positive feedback about my customer service skills.

The serious discussion ended with him offering me a raise and more responsibilities. I would travel between stores learning and doing more I could move me into a management position.

He finished by asking me to seriously consider his offer and to give him an answer in the next few days.

I ate in silence as he alternated between complimenting the food and complimenting me for a job well done.

I was skeptical of his motives and found it strange that this had all been done without my uncle present. It was an attractive offer but I was hesitant to make such a long-term commitment. This was his career path, not mine and in my heart I knew I couldn't work with him, or for him, for the rest of my life.

"Obviously, I'll have to discuss it with my parents tonight before I give you an answer," I finally replied wondering again why my uncle was not present at this meeting. "In fact, it will probably be easier if I go to your dad's store tomorrow too."

This would give me a chance to ask my uncle about this new arrangement and get some clarity on the decision.

"Of course, no problem," he replied almost too willingly. "You can have the rest of day off as well so you can think about. I'll call your folks to let them know. If you have all your stuff with you now I'll drop you at home when we are done here. Is that OK with you pal?"

Pal? I thought to myself, he never calls me pal. He had spoken to me more in the last hour than he had in the past few weeks. I knew he was planning something, I just didn't know what – yet.

"That's great, thank you." I answered without emotion and without sarcasm as I tried to figure out how my 'promotion' would benefit him. "I'll make your drive even shorter, would you drop me off at the library?"

"No problem." He flirted a bit more with the cashier as he paid. In the car he asked me if I minded listening to his music then turned it on to a tolerable volume. There had to be an underhanded, sneaky reason for this odd behavior and whatever it was would only end up helping him and hurting me. He was nothing like his father in this respect and I knew in my heart that it didn't feel right.

Chapter 16 ~ Intention - Lesson from Nature

He dropped me off at the library with a friendly goodbye and reminded me how excited he was for me to say yes to this great opportunity. I walked in, anxious to hear what Andrew had to say about this 'great opportunity' and my cousin's strange behavior before I spoke to my parents.

The head librarian told me that Andrew was doing some work outside when I enquired where he was.

He wasn't in the usual places so I walked around the building to find him. The storeroom door was open and I saw the light on as I entered. There were a few tools on the floor, which was rather unusual because I knew how neat he kept the place. I didn't see Andrew in there...right away.

I looked around the room then saw his shoes sticking out from behind the shelf on the far end of the wall. I walked over and found him lying on his side with a flashlight intensely looking at the floor at the base of the outside wall of the storeroom.

"Andrew, are you alright? What are you doing on the floor?"

"My brother, good to see you. Kunjani namhlanje? (How are you today?) Come look."

I knelt down to see what he was looking at and studying so intensely. "What are you looking for? Did you lose something down here?"

"No, No my brother" he replied laughing at my questions, "I am studying and learning from nature. Come look down here where I point the light, do you see them? Uyazibona iimbovane?"

"Sorry, you lost me on that one. Translation please."
Andrew smiled, "of course my brother. Uyazibona, do you see,
iimbovane, the ants. Do you see the ants?"

"Thank you for the translation, I didn't know that word,
iimbovane. Yes, I see the ants." I knew better than to simply start
telling him what was on my mind so I waited for him to continue. I
was sure there was a lesson coming though I couldn't imagine what
lesson ants could teach us. I stifled the sarcastic remark that came to
mind and opened my mind to my mentor and his wonderful,
strange way of teaching me life changing lessons.

"Yes sir, I see the ants." I repeated.
"What do you see down there," Andrew asked again.

"I see a line of ants. Would you like me to kill them for you?
I'm sure you have some chemical spray in here somewhere to get rid
of them." I turned and started walking toward the shelf with the
garden supplies. A quick spray would send them to their deaths
followed by sweeping away the resulting mess. I had done it many
times before and I would gladly do it for my friend today. How
strange that a gardener would be afraid of killing ants and would
ask me to do it instead. What if I had not been here today? He would
have had to face the scary ants himself.

"Ouch!" I screamed as I felt the pain. Andrew had walked
up behind me and slapped the back of my head. "What did you do
that for?"

"You were thinking again. I asked you a simple question
and before I could answer you, you walked off to do what you
'thought' I wanted. Am I right?"

"Yes," I replied sheepishly, "I was also wondering why you
of all people would be afraid to kill a line of ants. Yes, I was off on
my own mission before you had even answered me and I assumed I
knew what you wanted me to do. O.K. so let's start over. Yes, I saw
the ants you were pointing out to me. Now what?" I answered while
still rubbing the back of my head.

"I should come hit you again, maybe harder this time. Stop
thinking, it gets in the way of learning. Come look at the line of ants
again."

"You're right, I'm sorry. And when I say I'm sorry I truly mean it too." I followed him and knelt down next to him as he illuminated the ants again with his flashlight.

He laughed as I explained myself, knowing how he felt about the word sorry.

"Clear your mind and watch them carefully. Do you see how they all walk along the same line in a jam-packed two-way traffic lane? Each ant follows the trail of the one in front of her without question. Watch carefully and you'll see that every ant takes the exact same path, never straying. It does not matter if there is a shortcut or a quicker way to the destination; every single one of these dozens of ants follow the exact same path."

I observed the same pattern in the line of ants going in the opposite direction. Even though they were mere millimeters from each other, their paths never crossed because they were following in the exact same footsteps as the one before them.

It reminded of the children's game where we would form a line and play 'follow the leader'. The leader would say, "walk this way" and do a silly walk in a random direction and we would all have to mimic his walk and follow him over, under and into various obstacles, never straying or questioning his leadership. It was fascinating to see this in the animal world since I hadn't taken the time to observe ants this closely without getting upset and getting rid of them right away. I explained my observations to Andrew and his familiar smile spread across his face.

"Very good my brother, very good. Do you know why they follow one another that precisely? O.K. Let me explain to you. Before the whole army of ants arrives, a scout ant is sent out to find food. When the food is found, she goes back to the anthill to call the others, leaving a scent behind to mark the road. Each ant then follows the scent knowing that there is food ahead and is responsible for leaving the scent behind them for the next ant to follow."

"The ant does not question why she is following the crowd; she does not get into an argument about a taking a shortcut and she does not complain about the work that lies ahead. She simply follows the one before her along the same curving, long, meandering pathway in order to reach the food and carry it back for the benefit of the whole colony. Now watch how quickly I can disrupt them."

He took his finger and lightly wiped across an empty spot in their path. This simple gesture caused chaos in the line and sent the ants scampering around. By swiping his finger across their path, Andrew had wiped out the scent and caused confusion in the ranks. I watched as the ants frantically ran around seeking the scent again so they could get back on the path. After a few minutes they obviously found it. I watched them fall back in line and mindlessly follow each other on the exact same path again. I looked over to see where they were going. There was a dead insect on the floor and I watched as they climbed over the body then leave with a piece of it. Andrew explained how this was their duty and how dedicated and strong they were; able to lift many times their own body weight as they carried food home.

"There is good and there is bad in the life of an ant," Andrew continued explaining. "The ant fulfills its duty in life by being the best that they can be and by working together as a team for the benefit of all. The bad part is that an ant never questions whether there is a better way or a quicker way to get the job done. They follow each other mindlessly and are easily confused when the path is disrupted like I had done.

This is an example of group mentality and is what has kept us down for so long. The path of the oppressed people in this country has now been disrupted and we are no longer content to just follow along without question. The power to rise up and be different, be better and be stronger is here my brother. It doesn't matter if it's political or personal; the time has come to stop being a mindless ant. I only hope we are ready for the end result of what we have started."

I looked at the ants with fresh eyes and saw myself in his analogy. I was an ant. I was following along like everyone else in my world, without question and without thought. Sure, I had some nagging questions that would come up in my mind yet they were never strong enough to move me to action. At least not until now…when I was being asked to make a decision and forced to take a stand for something that would alter my life. How appropriate that it applied to both my school and my newly found work life. I questioned him further to see if I understood his message.

"OK, this is a great analogy and I think you are telling me that I made the right decision to boycott with my fellow students. It's amazing how your lesson applied to my exact situation. I also have a question about another situation that has come up. I don't know what you know about business but I'll ask for your opinion anyway."

"Hold on my brother, hold on. Did you say you were thinking again? You know that's what gets you in trouble or at least slapped behind your head by a gardener. This was not supposed to be a lesson specifically for you but since it seemed to apply to you let me continue with it. By the way you'll be surprised about how much I know about business. Anyway, hold on because you may only have heard what you wanted to hear in the story since you are looking for a specific answer."

"Humans are the smartest animal on earth and the only one with the capacity of thought, reasoning and logic. We take this wonderful gift and do amazing things. We invent items and objects to make our lives easier. We make our lives comfortable and convenient as we use our minds to benefit mankind. Isn't it great to have the ability to solve these complex problems that other animals cannot?"

He turned and waited for my answer. I nodded in agreement and he continued.

"On the other hand we also abuse this power of logic and comprehension. We use labels like manager or boss to hold someone back. We teach hatred and we see differences instead of similarities. We segregate and we systematically oppress and suppress those around us. We then legitimize our bad decisions by writing laws like Apartheid to inspire hatred and racism. When there is opposition we use our amazing brains to maintain power by inventing guns to keep those laws in place. Even though we know it is innately wrong we ignore logic and conscience and continue down the path of destruction. We use our inventions under the guise of law to kill each other and convince ourselves that it is a necessity in order to survive. We teach ourselves to think then we over-think ourselves into negativity and depression.

Yes, most people are ants and if it were not for what is happening now with the uprising we would still be ants. After this is over, I'm sure we will go back to being ants again unless you understand this lesson completely. Come with me."

We had stood up while we were speaking and he led me outside after putting his tools away.

"Come look up here," he said pointing to the top of the light post in the parking lot. "Do you see the beautiful spider web up there? Look over to the side of it and you'll see the spider patiently waiting. The spider works alone and is a seemingly smarter creature than the ant. She weaves her beautiful web in amazing almost, perfect places in order to catch her prey. How does she know where to place her web? Does she have an engineering degree and use calculus to determine the location and angle for the elaborate pattern and perfectly spaced rows? Does she ever complain about how much work it will take and the fact that she has to stay up all night jumping across long distances in order to finish her masterpiece needed for basic survival not aesthetics and beauty?

No, she innately does her spider duties without asking why because manifesting her spider-ness is what she was meant to do. You see, even though the spider is completely different from the ant they share many things in common."

The first one is that they do what needs to be done without question and without concern of the effort necessary to achieve what they want. The second thing is that they act innately without thinking. In human beings the first step, is the lesson from last time, the one you called Mindset.

After you have the right Mindset you have to have the right Intention. Intention is the ability to do what needs to be done regardless of the obstacles, the circumstances or the amount of work that it takes. Intention is the reason you take the actions and make the decisions that you do – it is the why, the purpose for doing something. Why are you joining the school boycott instead of staying in school? Why are you working right now? All actions my brother, are judged by intentions. All actions my brother, should be done with the right intention instead of the wrong emotion. Does that help you?"

"Not really, it confused me more." I had not been aware of my negative mindset before this. I was an ant, influenced by the notion, image and traits that my family, culture and surroundings had heaped upon me. I was locked with mental shackles and fooled into believing that I was free. My existence was simply to think, act and do what was expected of me in order to fit in, rather than stand up and risk standing out. Is that what my cousin was doing, turning me into an ant so I would follow blindly because of my label, or promotion as he called it and be kept in line by the paycheck?

Andrew, please help me understand." I was directly asking for his advice and pleading for help.

"If I am like the ant, I am simply following the crowd and doing what everyone else is doing. If I am like the spider I am all alone waiting on the sidelines for something to happen. I don't feel like I'm simply following along mindlessly like the ant anymore and I am definitely not alone like the spider because thousands of seniors are taking a stand and joining the boycott. Even being in the working world right now, people need jobs to earn money and survive in life. I thought I had made the right decision yet after listening to you I'm not sure if I have."

"Let me explain a bit more to you my brother. Both the ant and the spider have positive and negative qualities in their behavior. When I disrupt the path of the ants, they find it again and keep going – some would say this is a good thing because they do not give up easily. They help and guide each other to get the desired result. Your lesson here is teamwork and commitment. Even though the world may seem to be against you, you must have a team around you that supports and encourages you on your mission. When I destroy the spider web, she will spin another web or she may move on to a different place. This is called perseverance and you must be able to keep moving forward. Just because you have the right mindset does not guarantee success. It must be followed by Intention.

The intention of both the ant and the spider come from their instinct, or Mindset, and requires no thinking. Your web/your box/your frame, no matter what you call it, will be tested and broken and challenged throughout your life and you will want to give up many times.

You will experience agony and torture, maybe not physically like those who are being arrested, but mentally over and over again and it will be easier to give up than to keep suffering. You must, like the ant and the spider, be prepared to die for your cause. If you are prepared to die, even mentally, to help others then you are being selfless instead of selfish and you have the right intention. Now that doesn't mean you have to be involved politically in any way. There are students who are prepared to die for the cause yet are still in school because they feel that that is the way they can make a difference.

Your intention and therefore your actions should be based on being selfless not selfish. You must be true to yourself. It should feel right to you down to your soul. Embrace the fact that your voice and your actions can and will make a difference. You have the power to make a difference in someone's life, even though you may not realize it right now. Follow your passion doing what you love and the money will follow. As a student or an adult, whether male or female, young or old, doctor or gardener you are touching and changing lives on a daily basis. Someone is looking up to you for leadership and direction and you are their hero.

Never underestimate the power that you have just by being you. Stop looking for blessings outside yourself; you are a blessing to someone in the world right now. Wake up and live your life like the hero that you already are. You have choices and being proactive instead of reactive is the only way to wake up. The world does not owe you anything. You have to create your own future. All the answers you seek are within you; stop thinking and get out of your own way so you can hear the answers. If you cannot or do not feel it then you need to re-examine your intention before you take further action. Remember your Mindset determines outcome, your Intention determines action."

"There you are, we need you upstairs Andrew," a librarian had come over to get Andrew. I realized we had been chatting for a while and he had to get back to work. As always he had left me with much to contemplate.

"Thank you Andrew," I turned to the lady who had come looking for Andrew, "I'm sorry, it was my fault. " I apologized to her and took the blame so he could get back to work.

"No problem my brother. One more thing before you go. As you let these lessons percolate within you, do something mindless and listen for what comes through. Movement like dancing or stillness like meditation will help you too. Hamba Kakushle (Go well) my brother," he waved and followed her inside.

I walked home quickly, staying alert for any patrols that could be in the neighborhood. As I was walking into the house I felt something brush against my face. Jumping back in surprise as my hand reflexively wiped my face I looked around to see what had brushed against my face. As I looked up I saw a spider scurrying up an almost invisible broken strand toward the eave above the front door.

I unlocked the front door and stood in the doorway looking up to see what she would do. The spider reached the eave of the house, stopped for a few seconds to make sure the danger had passed then slid down a new thread that she attached to the downspout on the corner of the house. I watched her for a few more minutes before entering the house.

I realized that mom had not taken anything out for supper so I pulled my favorite meal from the freezer to thaw. Since I was going to surprise the family with supper I decided to cook my favorite meal for everyone.

I had much to contemplate so I turned on some music and started dancing around the house. Turning the offer down felt like the right decision after Andrew explained the power of intention. Yes, it felt right not to become an ant in my cousin's world and be stuck behind a counter. I knew mom would understand and I hoped that dad would too. Dad would have to understand I said out loud as I passed the kitchen counter.

I looked down at the thawing meal in the sink and thought of dad again. Even though it was my favorite meal dad didn't really care for it. The more I looked at it the clearer I remembered that dad did not like this meal. It was one of the few things I've heard him tell mom he didn't like.

Despite dad's parenting style he was a loving man to mom in his unique way and would always thank her for supper and tell her how tasty her food was except for this particular meal.

The old me would have been spiteful and cooked it anyway just to watch him suffer through it and to show him who was in charge. After hearing Andrew's explanation earlier I knew that I could not justify my action. Without further thought I replaced it.

It dawned on me that I had acted as the spider would act. I did what needed to be done without concern for myself. I had shifted my intention and with a loving mindset and taken action for the desired outcome. A feeling of calmness and gratitude came over me as the realization set in that I had been selfless and acted without letting my thoughts get in the way.

Speaking of spiders I opened the front door to check on the one I had disturbed earlier. There was no sign of her or her web by the front door. Curious to find out where she was, I walked around the house looking under the eaves. It wasn't until I was walking back to the front door that I saw her and her fully spun web in all its beauty glistening in the late autumn sun. The web was neatly spun from the trunk of a tree to its upper branches near the front of the house. She had moved to a completely different location, probably after I had interfered with her plans and ended up spinning her web in a better location. Was this instinct or did it require thought or intelligence?, I wondered. Of course not, Andrew was right; instinct in the animal world could be compared to mindset in humans with the right intention and actions to follow. Mindset determines outcome and intention determines actions.

I went back into the house and called my uncle. I would take care of it like an adult and speak to him first before I spoke to my parents. I was being a spider again. His friendly voice on the phone was calming to me and he didn't ask too many questions when I requested a meeting with him. I could hear the hesitation in his voice but he agreed without questioning me further.

I felt good as we sat at the table and enjoyed the meal I had prepared. Both mom and dad asked if I wanted to discuss anything because my cousin had called earlier and told them about his offer.

I explained that I wanted to discuss it with my uncle first and was spending the next day at his store then would chat with them afterward.

Surprisingly they agreed without pressuring me to open up about it and let the matter rest quickly. Could they really be starting to trust me more and see me as an adult because of all the changes I was making in my life?

I felt great and it seemed like they could feel it too.

Chapter 17 ~ Love & Forgiveness

Everything was great in my world as I quickly finished breakfast, cleaned my dishes and opened the front door to enjoy the brisk morning air as I waited for my uncle.

Winter would be here soon and so would mid-year exams if I had been at school. A small part of me still wondered about my school as the news about the boycotts and the clashes with police and army forces kept getting worse. I went to find a pen to make a note to call Peter to see what he could tell me. It seemed like I hadn't seen him in ages and I had grown so much in such a short time. Being away from school and the students gave me sense of comfort and protection since there were no political rallies at work.

The knock on the door was my uncle and I waved him in. I had not figured out how I was going to approach him yet so I avoided his direct questions during the ride. Fortunately I didn't have to stall for very long as he started picking up the others and they started chatting as well. I knew once we arrived at the store we would be busy and I'd have a chance to gather my thoughts before I spoke to him.

As expected, I was helping out pretty quickly and filled in wherever I was needed. It may have been my imagination but people seemed to be attracted to the new me and I found myself helping more customers than some of my co-workers.

Even while working, I would do mindless activities like stocking quickly to be less ant-like and take extra time and effort for what I saw as spider duties. I stayed busy and was unaware of how quickly the day was going until my uncle came over to get my attention.

"Come with me," he said before I could help another customer. He led me to his office and I smiled as I recognized the two sandwiches waiting on the table.

"Help yourself," he offered as he pointed to the table and pulled a chair up to his desk for me.

"What's on your mind?" he asked after I sat down. "You seem to be in a different world today. I'm not sure what it is but you are a different person from the doc I know. What is it?"

I took a bite of the tuna sandwich and debated on how much to share with him. I didn't want to start on a negative note so I probed further.

"Obviously, I have a lot on my mind right now. I'm sorry if it's affecting my work. I thought I was doing well today."

"Don't give me that crap; this is me you are talking to not your dad. You know I was saying the difference was positive not negative. What's your story?"

I smiled and continued eating. "Thank you for the sandwich. Yes, things are very different. The short version is that I've had an unlikely mentor for the last few weeks and he has taught me a lot about myself and about the world around me. I feel like I now have a better understanding and I'm not as confused as I was before. He has even helped me with an issue that has come up at the store"

"Anyone I know and what kind of problem at the store?" "I'll start with the positive news first. No, it's no one that you know. I don't think anyone really knows who he is. I know I have to get back to work so I'll be quick."

"Back to work hey?" He pushed the intercom button and summoned my cousin to the office.

"Yes dad," my cousin poked his head in the door. "He's in here with me if you're looking for him. I'll send him back out when we are done. O.K.?" He turned back to face me without waiting for an answer.

"We're really busy out there and we can use all the help we can get." His father had already turned to face me so he was speaking to the back of his head.

He glared at me in anger. "We really need you out here."

"Yes, as soon as we are done." My uncle repeated and waved him away without turning his head. As the door closed my uncle made eye contact with me again, "you were saying?"

I dismissed the angry stare my cousin had given me before he left and gathered my thoughts before answering my uncle's question. We tolerated each other because we were family but there was no love lost between us. I'm sure he was wondering what his father could possibly want from me that would warrant me getting out of work during the busy time.

"How much do you want to know?" I enquired. "Whatever you wish to share. You have a glow around you today and I noticed how busy you were earlier. Customers are attracted to you and I'd like to know what's going on so I could bottle what you have and sell it in the store? Geez, I'd make millions and split it with you. Seriously though, speak to me. I promise that nothing you tell me will leave this room."

I knew he would keep our conversation confidential but I was still hesitant about sharing with him. He had moved his chair out from behind his desk and was sitting right next to me. He leaned forward waiting for me to begin. His eyes sparkled and he seemed to look through me not at me. I could feel a warm energy coming from him, a strong feeling of caring and love. I had only felt this from one other person in my life – mom.

I leaned forward to face him and started at the very beginning. I shared my thoughts, my feelings and my fears. I told him what I had seen at the store and I told him about my lessons from all those around me. I kept sharing with him even though I was crying at times and laughing at some of the stories.

He listened intently, occasionally touching my leg to comfort me. After I was done, we both sat in silence for a few minutes.

The energy in the room had changed and I felt the air energize me and relax me at the same time. I looked over at my uncle who also appeared to be basking in it with a glow around his head too.

"Wow!" he finally said, "Wow!" He moved his chair and sat back staring at me. "You have had quite a ride in a short period of time.

It took me years to learn some of those lessons and I'm still working on teaching them to my boys. I'll deal with my son and what's been going on at that store. Don't worry; I shall not reveal my source. Now regarding this Andrew fellow, I'd like to meet him some day and let him know what an awesome job he has done. You remind me a lot of me when I was your age. I've achieved quite a bit in my life so far though I wish I had known what you know now when I was that young. I'm still learning and I know my boys are nowhere close to where you are. Don't get me wrong, I love my boys but their mindset…" He stopped and looked at me, wiping away tears.

"I'm just so proud of you." He walked over and gave me a hug. Surprisingly, I winced in pain as he squeezed me tightly. I ignored the pain as my eyes filled with tears again. We were equals, two men unafraid to share their feelings and show love. Why couldn't dad be this way?

The intercom on his phone buzzed again and brought us back to the present. He had ignored it twice while I was speaking and he reached over to answer it now.

"Yes. Tell him to hold, I'll take the call. Sorry, I have to take this call. Go ahead and head back to the floor when you are ready. I'll see you there."

I was glad he turned away to pick up the phone so he didn't see me limp out his office. The pain in my back and hips was getting worse and going down my right leg. Even my toes were tingling but I felt too good after sharing everything with him to let the pain bring me down.

I ignored the looks I was getting from my cousin and went back to helping customers. Fortunately we stayed busy and he didn't have time to stop and speak to me. He passed me at one point and whispered, "Why are you kissing up to the old man?" and walked off before I replied. Even with the right mindset I wondered why things could not have been different. If only he saw his dad the way I did and if only my dad could see me the way my uncle did.

"Stop thinking. Stop thinking," Andrew's voice came to mind, as I was lost in thought stocking the shelves.

"Ewe (yes)," I said out loud.

"Yes, what? Yes it's time to go home." My co-worker had been stocking the next aisle and answered me.

I laughed, "Great. Thanks." I struggled to my feet and went to find my uncle, doing my best to avoid my cousin. I did not see him and after asking someone about him heard that my uncle had asked him to drop off the employees so he could take me home. The reason became clear after everything we locked and were alone in the car.

"Thank you for sharing with me today," he started saying as we entered the highway. "I'd like to add something to what your friend Andrew has taught you. I'm sure he'll be getting to this at some point but I want to tell you now. Do you mind?"

"No, of course not, I would be honored." I felt closer to him than ever before and I was happy that someone else could share what I was going through. This must be the teamwork principle that Andrew had spoken about.

"Prayers," he blurted out and looked over at me. "Prayers are important. Ask for help from a higher power and keep positive self talk going all day long. If you don't like that word then call it positive self-talk or positive affirmations. You will be challenged, by people and by circumstances around you, throughout your life and you need to persevere. Affirmations and prayers will keep you going when the world seems to be crashing around you. The people who love and care about you the most will be the ones who hold you back. Accept that fact and keep moving forward with intention. Nothing and I mean nothing, will come your way that you cannot handle. Bad things happen to good people and vice versa, so be careful about questioning and judging the event. No matter what, learn and grow from every experience.

Use these when you feel down, when you feel all alone, when you are in doubt and also when everything is going well. Ask for guidance not for a wish list to be fulfilled.

There is a right way and a wrong way to do affirmations though. The right way is to always make it a positive statement in the present tense. Your subconscious mind, the one responsible for your mindset, has no concept of time.

Whether you experience an event in person or you imagine a situation, your subconscious mind will accept it. I was successful and had a busy store long before I left the military.

All day, every day, I saw it in my mind and when it happened in real life it was simply the physical manifestation of what I had already experienced in my mind.

Use these with what Andrew has taught you and you'll be amazed at how far reaching it will be. You have a voice, you have a talent and you will touch many lives. I've known that for a long time doc, I've known it for a long time. Do what you want to do for yourself, that is intention. Do it for you not for your parents, not for me, not for them – whoever *they* may be. Do it for yourself – always. You must be a little selfish with your intention initially so you can reach the point of selflessness that Andrew has taught you. Any question on this doc?"

"No, not yet. It all makes sense so far. Just like Andrew, you guys make it sound so easy. Why am I carrying this huge burden then? I must be an ant. I'm too young for all this."

He laughed. "You are not an ant. You never have been. Without mentioning any names, I can tell you with certainty that there are many ants in the family. Watch and listen and you'll know who they are. The ants are the ones who get scared when you dare to be different and go off and create your own path. Yes, there are a few spiders in the family too but they are the quiet ones; watching, learning and admiring you from afar."

I giggled at the thought, "ants in the family" I repeated. "Would you give me names or at least hints as to who they are?"

"Ha! You wish. No, I'll do better than that. I'll tell you how to ignore their negativity. It comes down to two words. The first one is LOVE! You must love yourself first. Everything that Andrew has taught you, starting with clearing your mind all the way to having the right intention starts with love.

When it comes to moving forward in life you call it passion or commitment, same thing, it comes back to love. When it comes to family, you really have to love them more to stop them from holding you back.

They will tell you how crazy you are and how naïve or foolish you are and how much of a dreamer you are all in the name of love.

Keep loving them and that's where number two comes in as well FORGIVENESS! You must love and you must forgive. Two ageless principles from the good books that we all know yet hardly apply to our lives. No matter what it is?

Love and forgiveness plus prayer and affirmation will get you back on track and keep you there."

We had been sitting in the driveway as he finished his explanation. The ride had gone much quicker since we had no other stops to make. I felt like the happiest, most loved person on earth. I had people who cared; cared enough to teach me and to help me become a better person. Nothing could go wrong in my life when I was surrounded by love even if dad did not agree with me. In his own way, I knew he loved me.

"Thank you. I really cannot thank you enough for everything you are doing for me and for us. I appreciate it all."

"No problem. You'll do the same for someone else someday. You said it perfectly earlier today Mindset Determines Outcome. You can handle it. What is she doing out here?" There was a knock on the car window. I turned and rolled the window down.

"Hi guys. How long have you been out here? Are you coming in for supper or at least for tea?" Mom must have seen us in the driveway and wondered why we had not come in to the house yet.

"No, thank you dear. I'm heading home," my uncle answered and turned back to me, "I'm proud of you, keep it going."

"Thank you. Ouch!" I had been sitting in the passenger seat facing the drivers' side while we chatted and now I couldn't move. My back was in spasm and I was in pain.

"What's the matter?" two voices asked in unison. "It's my back. I cannot move. No, don't open the door mom. I'm stuck and it hurts. What should I do?"

"Calm down, it's just a back spasm," I heard my uncle say as mom started panicking. I could hear them talking outside the car and I couldn't turn to see what was going on.

"Ok. Ok. You'll be Ok." Mom had slid into the driver's seat and was now attempting to calm me down. "What do you need?"

"I don't know mom, I've never had this before. What should I do? Where did he go? Maybe if I go lie down for a while it will relax."

"Stay calm and don't move. He said he knew what to do and he went inside to make some phone calls. Will you be alright for a few minutes while I go see what he found out?'

"Yes. I'll be right here," I answered sarcastically trying not to move too much. They both returned a few minutes later and mom got in the backseat.

My uncle closed her door for her before returning to the driver seat and starting the car.

"OK, let's go," he said as he pulled out of the driveway. "Where are we going? I'm sure resting for a while will make it better." I was still facing the drivers side and it felt strange not seeing the road. I wondered if mom had convinced him to take me to the hospital. That would be the only logical place to go.

Even though I was in pain I found it quite amusing that I probably knew the names of the bones and muscles involved in my pain. Perhaps saying it out loud would convince them to take me back home and to bed. "It's only a spasm in the lumbar and sacrum area you know. The piriformis and gluteus muscles will relax when I rest. It's probably just a mild sprain and strain from all the activity over the last few weeks. There's no need to go to the hospital."

"That's sounds good doc," my uncle chimed in. "I have no idea what you said but it sounded good. What I do know is that rest will not help you. Believe me! I've had this happen to me many times before. We are not going to the hospital either, they will only give you muscle relaxers. I'm taking you to my doctor who will fix you right up like he's done for me so many times. I caught him as he was leaving his office and he said he would wait for us."

Chapter 18 ~ The Pivotal Life Changing Event

"You'll be fine dear," mom chimed in from the back seat trying to comfort me. "It's nothing serious. Well, I hope not, is it?" That sounded like a question for my uncle and it was one I had as well. What the heck was going on with me and was it serious? "Nope, nothing serious. This guy is good and he'll fix you right up.

Here we are." He parked and walked around to my side of the car. "Lean forward slightly," he said and opened the door slowly. I felt two sets of hands reach in and lift me by the leg and the shoulder. My screams of pain were ignored as I was lifted up and out of the car and into a wheelchair. Someone else was pushing me and it was too painful to turn to see who it was.

My uncle held the door open as mom entered and I rolled in, the wheelchair being pushed by Mr. or Ms. unknown.

We had entered a brightly painted office with a desk in front of us. Mom headed to the desk and was signing papers as we turned left and walked past some toys and crayon drawings on the wall. We were now in an open space with four tables in arranged in a star shape formation. They looked like tables but were low and narrow like a bed. My wheelchair stopped in front of one of these and Mr. Stranger came around and stood in front of me.

"Welcome to Green Park Chiropractic Centre, I'm Dr. Ray. Good to meet you sir. Now let's see if we can help you, shall we? I'll help you out of the chair if you can slide onto the adjusting table and lie on your side, whichever side is comfortable for you.

Here's a pillow for your head and one to go between your legs once we get you down. OK, here we go. Take your time; I know it hurts, easy does it."

The pain in my low back and hips was an intense throbbing going down my right leg to my toes.

It felt like I was being jabbed in my hip with a sharp, hot metal rod every few seconds. Leaning forward and to the side eased the pain slightly except when I took deep breaths. Even though the wheelchair was right in front of the table it seemed far when measured in painful, jabbing steps. I pushed myself up and out of the chair and collapsed right back into the chair in pain. I had just discovered how excruciating it was to stand or put weight on my right leg.

"Take your time," Dr. Ray said as he lifted me slightly to take the weight off my leg and move me closer to the table. My uncle came over and between them managed to push, shove and wiggle me onto the table and get the wheelchair out of the way. It felt good to lie on my side with a pillow between my legs.

"So! What seems to be the problem young man? Tell me what happened." Dr. Ray was on a rolling stool in front of me with a clipboard and a pen.

"He's got a pain in his bum doc," my uncle said laughing, "must be his parents, I've always known they were a pain in the rear and now it shows."

"Not funny. It hurts to laugh. Stop it." I cried out in pain. "He's right though doc, that is where it hurts. The pain also goes down my right leg and my toes tingle all the time."

"When did it start? Do you recall a fall or other type of injury?" Dr. Ray started asking a series of questions. I answered them all and asked a few along the way as well. Of course, I avoided embarrassing myself by leaving out the exact details of my vacuum cleaner fall. After taking notes on his clipboard he put it aside and rolled around on his stool to the back of me. I felt his hands gently feel my spine. Then he moved up the spine to the back of my head and neck then down again to my hips.

"This is where the magic happens," my uncle came into view in front of me while the doctor kept checking other areas. "Now you get to experience the magic of healing hands," my uncle repeated as he looked over at the doc behind me.

"Really," I heard him say. "Already? O.K. If you say so." He turned his attention back to me. "Get up. Come on, get up."

"Wait, what do you mean get up. Do you realize what it took to get down here? And besides, the doc hasn't done anything yet."

I felt the doctor's hand on my shoulder and knew he was still sitting behind me. "Yes, I'm done. You can get up now. Slowly though, O.K.?"

"Are you serious? Get up by myself, right now?"

"Yes, sir. All the way up," Dr. Ray repeated.

I looked over at my uncle who had a broad smile on his face and was nodding his head gesturing me to get up.

"Take my hand," he said and stepped forward.

I took a shallow breath and exhaled slowly in anticipation of the waves of pain that would inevitably knock me down again. I pushed up slightly, then with much trepidation, pushed further.

My uncle was helping pull me up and I was pushing myself up with the other hand. I closed my eyes tightly, bracing myself, again waiting for the pain to return. It didn't.

OK, that was lucky I thought as I came up into a seated position. It was sore and tender but not throbbing like before.

"No, all the way. Go ahead. You can stand and you can walk. There will be a little discomfort though it shouldn't stop you from walking." Dr. Ray sounded confident and sincere in his statement. There was no doubt in his voice.

I pulled my uncle closer and hung on to his arm as I stood up. I trusted the doctor but still wanted to be cautious about putting weight on my right leg. "Whoa! No way," was all I could say as I stood up all the way with equal weight on both legs. I held on to him as I took my first step then soon realized that I was strong enough to do it by myself. I could walk almost completely upright and mostly pain free. "No way. No way," I kept repeating over and over again as I took more steps. I heard a shriek from mom as she looked in and saw me walking.

"Do you feel anything?" she asked as she came over to walk with me.

"I feel great. I feel like I'm dreaming right now because there's no pain and believe me *there was* pain. I feel great, I really do. Where have you been mom?"

"I was doing the paperwork for you. Dr. Ray said he would get started with you right away instead of waiting for me to finish. I just had to give him permission and sign one page so he could start. Do you really feel better?"

"Not just better mom, I feel great. It's sore and achy but great compared to what it was before." I looked over to Dr. Ray and to my uncle who were both smiling. "How did you do that?"

"That's the power of the chiropractic adjustment. The power that made the body heals the body." Dr. Ray had only spoken a few yet powerful words with results to prove it. He sounded a lot like mom, my uncle and Andrew.

"Tell me more. How did you do that? This is not an illusion, what I'm feeling or rather not feeling is real. Can anyone do this?"

"Never underestimate the power of the human mind and the human body. Here, take this brochure and read about it. Bring him back in two days for another adjustment and we'll chat more then. Ice that low back for thirty minutes when you get home."

"Yes, one of us will bring him." I heard mom say. "You have his mind rolling doctor. Thank you so much for staying late to see us."

I was standing a few feet away as she was speaking to Dr. Ray waiting to go back to the car. What happened next is impossible to explain. It was like me watching me do what I did and not being able to stop myself.

"This is what *I* want to do. Mom, can I be a chiropractor?"

I had blurted it out loud enough for mom, my uncle and Dr. Ray to hear and it surprised everyone, including me. The realization of what I had just verbalized hit me, about the same time as everyone else but it was too late to take it back. I started to think about what I had said. It had not been me speaking, it was like my brain had been taken over and someone else had spoken.

What the heck was I thinking? I realized that I wasn't thinking, simply verbalizing what had to be. I was being called from deep within to follow this path. This would be my legacy.

Mom spoke first, "What did you say?"
In my mind I was asking that same question. I had no desire to go to university. In fact, not only did I have no desire, I didn't have the grades either. Reality set in and I hesitated before I spoke.

Dr. Ray spoke before I had a chance to take back my bold announcement. "I think it's a great idea. There are no coloured chiropractors in Cape Town so you can be the first. Are you a senior right now?"

"Yes he is," mom answered then turned to face me.
 "Yes, you can. If that's what you want do, of course you can. Dr. Ray, how do we do that? Where can I get more information?"

"I'll have the information ready for you next time. Is that OK? Wow! This is very exciting; you want to be a chiropractor. Cool!" he mumbled mostly to himself. He came over to hug me.

I hugged him back without saying anything else; partially to thank him for getting me out of pain and partially because I was speechless at what had just transpired.

"O.K., you two off to the car, I'll be right there. Thanks again doc," my uncle said and went to shake Dr. Ray's hand as mom and I walked out to the car. I still couldn't believe what had happened AND that I was feeling so good after the visit.

He joined us in the car and we headed home in the dark. "I told you he would fix you right up didn't I?" he said as we drove. "I just did it so you wouldn't miss a day of work," he joked as he dropped us off at home. "Get some rest and sleep in a bit. I'll come by after lunch to pick you up." He looked at mom, "Dr. Ray said he could work tomorrow. I'll come get him after lunch then keep him with me at my store to make sure he doesn't do any heavy lifting. Is that alright with you?"

"That would be great, thank you. You don't have to do that though. I've already called in to work so I could stay with him in the morning. I don't want to disrupt your schedule." Mom offered.

"No ma'am, I insist." my uncle shot back.

"Excellent, thanks," then she turned to me "you can sleep in tomorrow then."

My dad and my brother were waiting for us when we walked in.

"Are you alright?" dad asked. "You had us worried there for a little while."

"Yes, I'm much better now, thank you. Can I go lie down?" "Here take some ice with you. Wrap it in a towel and put in on your low back. Are you hungry?" mom asked as she led me to the kitchen.

"Ice yes, thank you. No, I'm going straight to bed." I had never lain on ice before and it felt strange and uncomfortable at first. It wasn't as cold as I thought it would be and I felt the relaxation effect on my muscles pretty quickly. I read his brochure and was soon drifting off to sleep. I thought I heard both mom and dad come in at various times to check on me. At some point I felt someone roll me over to remove the bag of melted ice from under me.

Chapter 19 ~ Applying the Lessons

I awoke early feeling refreshed and mostly pain free. I had slept well and was surprised to see that I had awoken so early. There was a little stiffness in my hips, which dissipated, after my shower and some light stretching. I felt invigorated and ready for the world, which I attributed to feeling great physically and to expanding my mental frame as I saw the world differently.

As I was getting dressed I heard my out-of-body announcement come back stronger, "I want to be a chiropractor." The voice in my head was my own and was making the announcement loudly and confidently, like it was a fact that had to be broadcast again so it could be heard. The new me recognized this as being due to my inner voice, my mindset shift, simply expanding my mental frame and I knew it wouldn't go away.

I knew I either had to prove to myself that it could be done or disprove it and convince myself that it was simply an impossible dream.

I pulled out a notebook and pen from my book bag that was gathering dust since I hadn't touched it in weeks and started writing. Across the top of the first page I wrote the burning question in big, bold capital block letters:

CAN I REALLY BECOME A CHIROPRACTOR?

Regardless of my current obstacles, including not having the grades or the money for college, I started writing. When a negative thought surfaced I wrote it down on a separate sheet and kept going.

Initially it felt like simply a pipe dream yet as I continued putting my free flowing ideas down in ink I came up with solutions in the process.

"Good morning darling. I'm surprised to see you up so early, I thought you'd be sleeping in this morning. How are you feeling?" Mom asked as she came up behind me and saw me writing at the kitchen table.

"What are you working on? It looks like you haven't even had breakfast yet. What would you like to eat? How long have you been up?" She leaned over my shoulder to see what I was writing as she brought me a glass of juice.

"Yes, of course you can," she said as she read the title.

"Can what?" Dad had come into the kitchen and overheard her. "Morning, how are you feeling?" he asked me then turned back to her, "yes, he can what?"

'Yes, he can be a chiropractor if that's what he wants to do," she said confidently to both dad and to me.

"Yes, about that mom," I stopped writing and turned around in my chair.

"Yes, about that?" dad repeated. "Your mom told me about your outburst in the doctor's office last night. Are you feeling better today, physically I mean?"

I was surprised that he was speaking to me. He actually sounded sincere and I detected a caring tone in his voice. Even his face was relaxed when he asked about my wellbeing. It was strange for me to hear this from the man that I had feared for so long. Was it my imagination or my new positive mindset?

This was my moment of truth to share what had emerged from my writing all morning. The last few lessons from Andrew and the conversations with my uncle are what had led to my outburst in the office. I was now at a turning point that made the decision inevitable. I could feel that a new chapter of my life was about to be written. The old me would have dismissed it all and gone back to my comfortable existence but that person was long gone. Experiencing excruciating pain and facing death by a soldier has a way of changing how you view life.

I had rehearsed what I wanted to say yet now my mind was going blank and my throat was dry. I had to share a tough decision with mom and with dad - the man who only communicated through discipline and fear as his parenting tool.

I cleared my throat and reached for my juice. It felt good to wet my throat and gave me a chance to gather my thoughts and calm myself down. Outwardly I was calm and I was grateful that they could not hear my heart thumping.

"After being in pain for a few weeks now and not letting you know about it," I started saying then took another sip of juice before I continued, "and experiencing the unbelievable results last night, I blurted out what I did because the pain was gone and I felt good. As I reflected this morning on what I had said, it became clearer to me that I had sincerely meant every word of it and it wasn't simply an emotional outburst." I paused and waited for a response, studying their faces and mentally preparing for a reaction from dad.

They looked at each other without saying a word then looked back at me in silence, waiting for me to continue. I was momentarily taken aback by their silence and dismissed the 'what kind of game are they playing?' thought that initially came up.

"Mom, Dad. I was serious about what I said. I want to change lives like Dr. Ray changed mine last night and I want to do what he does every day. The first step is the obvious one, despite what I had said a few weeks ago. I'm glad to say that I have no choice in the matter because it has to be this way. *I'm going back to school* so I can graduate and get to college or whatever I need to do to make it happen. I'll find out what I need to do to get back to school and how to get the schoolwork. Mom, you said you trusted me to make my own decision and I know that…"

"No," mom interrupted me loudly. "No, you are not going back to school."

"Excuse me! Mom, what do you mean no?" obviously shocked by her response. She seemed adamant with her response yet dad was smiling and not saying anything.

"Your father and I discussed it last night and we will not allow it," she continued.

"What happened to letting me make my own decision and supporting me in what I wanted to do?" I couldn't believe what I was hearing from my own mother whom I thought was supporting me. A small part of me was actually hoping that dad would be on my side, though I didn't realistically see any chance of that being true. In fact, he was walking out of the kitchen while I was speaking. "Mom, I thought you had said…"

"Let me finish," she interjected again, "your dad and I knew that you would reach this decision if you were serious about what you said and we are excited to hear you say it. We agree with your decision but we disagree with you going back to school, the physical school, because it's much too dangerous for you there. You've been acting strangely lately and I knew something was brewing inside that head of yours. I know you too well for you to hide anything from me so I made some calls last week and we have a solution. In fact, you had mentioned it before and we had all forgotten about it until now. I called your teachers and they have agreed to provide what you need to prepare for the exams.

They are making arrangements for the upcoming midterms for the students not wanting to take them at school. Study groups are forming now at students and teachers houses at night and on weekends. It will be hard work but it can be done if this is what you want to do. You can study at work although you'll have to put in a lot of study time to catch up and stay current."

Intention determines action, I thought before I answered. "Yes I know it will be hard. I know it's going to be tough and I have a lot of catching up to do yet it needs to be done. I will do whatever it takes to finish school. I can no longer settle for less. I made a commitment today and I have to honor that commitment. Geez! You scared me when you said no earlier."

Mom smiled, "I know. You'll get it. You should have seen your face when I cut you off mid sentence."

Dad had returned to the kitchen and smiled when he saw us chatting. "You can get started right now. You feel good and you're not working till this afternoon right?" He said as he handed me three thick folders.

"Here's what you need to get up to date in your first three subjects. Your mom picked these up last week. You'll have the work for your other three subjects in a few days. We'll double check with Mr. Petersen but I believe you have about three weeks to catch up in all your subjects before the midterms. Your teachers have included their phone numbers if you need to call them. There are study groups every night but we need to call after four to find out where they are meeting for the night. The location is only given to the people who call and is changed every night to reduce the chance of the police showing up."

"Oh wow. Thank you both." I said as I took the folders and starting flipping through them. Admittedly it seemed like a daunting task yet I was looking forward to the challenge.

"I *will* get started right away. Again thank you for your understanding."

Mom spoke again. "We love you and we want what's best for you. Not for our sake, for yours. Tell us what you need and we'll do what we can. Promise me you'll ask us for help when and if you need it." Mom had tears in her eyes as she spoke. "We are proud of you for taking a stand and for making these life changing decisions. I, no we, support you and we love you."

Dad was nodding as she spoke. It was the first time in my life that he was agreeing and not controlling the conversation.

"Yes, we are very proud of you," dad said with tears in his eyes too.

I had faced the man I feared for a second time and I had made a surprising discovery, my dad was human. The man had feelings. The toughest disciplinarian in the world, the man who would not spend money on anything, had taken me seriously and agreed to help. He was a strong, proud man and I had somehow managed to get through to him. He walked over and shook my hand cupping it with both of his, smiled, then turned and walked out. This was the equivalent of a loving hug from dad and I appreciated his heartfelt gesture.

I had a lot of studying to do before work and life was great. I was moving forward with an expanded mental frame.

"Get out of here with all that schoolwork, I'll get breakfast going. Are you going to your room?"

"Yes mom, I'll be in my room studying. And thank you, for everything."

"You still have to do dishes before you go though because I have to leave before you do this afternoon."

I headed up to my room with my folders to start studying.

Dad opened my door a few minutes later to say goodbye as he left for work and mom came in soon afterwards with a hearty breakfast.

I kept reading while I ate, determined to get some good study time before my uncle picked me up for work. I was moving forward with an expanded mental frame, a positive mindset and the right intention. Life was looking good.

I started with my favorite subject, Xhosa.

My uncle arrived just after noon with two sandwiches and a drink for both of us. I was surprised to see him in a blue button down shirt and tie.

"What's the occasion?" I asked as I opened the front door, "Should I dress up too?"

"No, no. I just felt like dressing up today. I've never worn this shirt before. It's been hanging in my wardrobe for a long time and today it called out to me. Don't get used it though, it won't happen again. Your mom called before she left and told me what was going on so I brought lunch for us. Congrats man, or should I say doc? I'm proud of you. I'm not too happy for me but I am excited for you. I've made some arrangements with the boys to help you out. How do you feel today?"

"I feel great, thanks. I slept well and I'm ready for work. What kind of arrangements?"

"Glad to hear that you're feeling better. I told you he would fix you up. Don't worry about the arrangements I've made, we can chat about that later. Light duty today, do you hear me? Light duty today. No heavy lifting. You stay at the register all day if you need to. Your cousin is just about ready run the place now but I still have some clout."

He winked at me and smiled, "why do you think I haven't let him move into my office yet. Yep, it's still MY office. Let's eat so we can get going. I have to pick up a few guys on the way back to the main store."

"Thank you kind sir, how very thoughtful of you. Would you like a glass for your drink or are you going to be rude and crude and drink from the bottle?" My sarcasm came out because I was in such a good mood and he felt it too.

"I'm not only going to drink from the bottle, I'm going to burp in your face later. You're a student again not the king of the country you know," he shot back as we ate in the kitchen.

We were on the road pretty quickly and continued with light conversation as we picked up a few workers along the way. I found it amusing that he kept having to explain why he was all dressed up over and over again to each employee as they got in to the van.

"It looks like you are going to a funeral or a wedding boss," someone had remarked and we all laughed.

My uncle took it all in stride and had sarcastic comebacks for everyone. We all knew we could joke around with him until he became 'the boss' when we were on the clock.

As expected the store was busy when we arrived. We all clocked in and I took over at the register. I stayed busy there yet still stepping in to stock and clean as needed without doing any heavy lifting. I even found a way to stretch while I checked people out all afternoon and had only minor stiffness. It felt good to be working with my uncle again instead of my cousin although I knew I couldn't stay at this store. I would have to face my cousin and stand up to him like I had done with the other major issues so far. Heck, after facing dad and seeing the results, my cousin was small fry. I found the thought amusing as I pictured myself with a baited fishing pole.

"What do I need to do to get good service in this place?" I heard a woman say loudly and smiled as I recognized her voice.

"Hi mom, what are you doing here?" I stepped out and gave her a hug.

"It's almost closing time and I needed some things," she replied, "and besides, I came to check on my patient. Did you do alright today?"

"Yes, thank you. I was at the register on 'light-duty' all afternoon and even managed to do some stretching back here."

"Can I take you home with me young man? You're a handsome one, how about I take you out when you get off work tonight?" she said in her best acting voice.

"Yes ma'am, it's a date. What will your husband think of that?" I responded playfully.

"We just won't tell him," she laughed and walked off to get her groceries. I heard her scream as she turned down an aisle. I looked over and saw my uncle next to her. Who knows what he did to her to make her scream. They were soon in conversation and he helped her shop. A few minutes later they walked up to me with a full cart of groceries.

"You get ready to go and I'll check her out." he said and stepped behind the register. I watched for a moment and saw him manually ring up a fraction of the actual cost for each item instead of the full price. I heard mom ask about the low final total when he was done. I heard him explain, in a serious tone, that he could only collect the amount that the register showed or he would get in trouble with his boss.

"Go clock out so you can go on a date with your mom," he said to me as I came back out to help carry the groceries. "Get outta here," he said as he shooed us out the door.

"Thank you. I'm not going to argue. It's been an interesting and amazing few days and now I get to go on a date with this lovely lady. Where shall we go?"

Mom smiled mischievously and started driving, "we'll figure out something," she said.

Mom had planned a full evening of Saturday activities for us. Dad had to work late so he wouldn't be joining us. We stopped at home, unloaded the groceries, picked up my brother then headed out on the town. We started at the mall then to a restaurant then to a movie of our choice. On the way home we even stopped for ice cream. My brother and I couldn't believe that she allowed us to eat ice cream this late at night.

It was well after dark when we arrived home, tired and happy after a busy day. Dad was in bed already and we quietly snuck in. I lay in bed being thankful for all I had and drifted off to sleep.

Chapter 20 ~ The Big Test

I was awakened by the ringing telephone echoing in the quiet house. I glanced at the clock and saw that it was after one.

A call this late could not be good. A few minutes later my bedroom door flung open and dad, half dressed, flipped the light on.

"Get dressed and grab a jacket. We have to go. NOW!" he screamed and left hurriedly. All the lights were on and mom was downstairs pacing and mumbling under her breath. Her face was a mess and I could tell that she had been crying. She was holding back the tears and it sounded like she was praying as she paced back and forth. Dad kissed her then turned to me.

"Let's go." I followed him to the car just as my yawning brother was speaking to mom.

He had already started the car and peeled out of the driveway without saying a word. I had never seen him like this, totally focused on the road and speeding through town. He would slow down at a red light, then cross it without waiting for it to change if there were no other cars around. The roads were deserted and I soon realized that we were going to the main store.

My adrenaline was pumping and my heart was racing, crazy thoughts running through my head yet too afraid to ask what was going on. A few blocks from the store, before we could even see the building, I saw the reflections in the windows of the stores along the road. The flashing lights of emergency vehicles reflected brightly in the dark. We could hardly turn the corner, because there were so many vehicles parked in front of the store.

Dad parked quickly and was soon sprinting toward the front door. I followed as quickly as I could, doing my best to dismiss the rampant thoughts of what could have happened.

Blinded by all the lights, I made it through the vehicles haphazardly parked along the way with their lights flashing and saw dad freeze as the store came in to view. He took a deep breath, and then slowly walked toward the front door of the store. I caught up to him to see what he was looking at. A loud audible gasp escaped my lips at what I saw.

The store was completely lit up and outside the threshold of the front door; I saw what dad had seen. Even from this distance, we knew. My body immediately felt numb and cold and my feet grew heavy and unable to move. I felt stuck where I stood. My eyes blurred as if in disbelief then refocused as my subconscious mind jolted me with the realization that what I was seeing was real.

We were stopped before we could get closer then allowed to cross the yellow taped off area after dad introduced himself to the officer.

"May we go see him?" I heard dad ask the uniformed officer without really waiting for an answer.

"As long as you don't touch the body sir. I'm sorry for your loss, sir. He was a good man, I knew him from his days on the force."

I gasped again in disbelief when I was finally able to will my feet to move and take me closer to the scene.

The contorted body of my uncle lay face down in a dark pool of blood just outside the front door of the store. His head was turned to the right; his nose bloody and twisted at an odd angle. In his left hand his index finger was still on the trigger of his gun, a flashlight close to his body on the right. There was so much blood on his head and body that it looked fake, like the blood I'd seen in novelty stores except much darker.

Dad was down on his knees, kneeling as close to my uncle as he could. He closed his eyes; his lips moving as he silently recited a prayer, tears rolling down his cheeks as his head bobbed while he sobbed.

I joined dad in silent prayer, kneeling to the right of him while we contained our sobs as best as we could.

He looked up as his name was called, briefly hesitating and not wanting to leave my uncle's side. It was my aunt and younger cousin who had just arrived.

Dad and I had been the first to arrive and we saw more family members arriving behind them. He walked over to her and they hugged in silence. "You may not want to see him like this," he whispered in her ear, "It's up to you."

I walked back to the front door of the store and was joined by another uncle and cousin. We looked down in silence, in shock and disbelief to see a man that we loved taken from us in such a violent manner. It was surreal, like a dream that we would awaken from at any minute yet there he was, intermittently being lit up by the flash of the crime photographer's camera.

"I shot one of them, I know I did." I heard my cousin explain to a gentleman who was taking notes in his little book. I had watched enough movies to know that he was a detective.

The detective approached all the family members and we were led into my uncle's office. The sounds us freely sobbing, crying and blowing noses echoed and reverberated. I had just been in here earlier I kept thinking, just a few hours ago. How could things change so quickly…and why? My day had started so well and now this. Why would a loving GOD let this happen to a good man?

"Ladies and gentleman. Excuse me ladies and gentleman," I heard an unfamiliar voice say. "Ladies and gentleman, my name is Detective Swanz. I'm sorry for your loss but I'd like to take a moment to let you know what we know so far."

Detective Swanz explained that after closing time, my uncle and cousin had gone to the back of the store to close out the registers and monthly balance. Since it was the end of the month, it was not unusual for them to stay overnight as they took inventory and stocked the shelves with a few employees. At some point, they heard a scream from the front of the store. One of the guys had propped the front door open for some fresh air, when three armed men entered, held a gun to his head and demanded money.

My uncle was the first one to hear the scream. He looked out and realized what was happening. Instinctively, he drew his weapon that was always on his belt, ordered my cousin to get the gun that was in his office and ran to the front of the store.

He instructed the worker to hit the floor, shouted a verbal warning, then ran forward and fired. The thieves were carrying automatic rifles and fired at him as he approached.

My cousin came up behind him and fired as they were fleeing just in time to see his father stumble and fall just outside the front door.

According to the preliminary findings he was hit twice, once in the heart and once in the head. The 'consolation' was that he had probably not felt any pain and was dead before he hit the ground. My cousin nodded and confirmed that his dad was no longer alive by the time he reached him just a few seconds later.

There was a trail of blood outside the front door in the direction of the parking lot indicating that one of the robbers may be injured. The employee's life had been saved by my uncle's quick action and was taken to hospital for minor cuts and bruises.

It appears that they did not have time to grab any money before they fled. He finished by reiterating what a senseless, tragic event it was and again offered his condolences for our loss. He answered most of our questions with "we'll know more after the investigation," then asked us to leave so they could continue at the crime scene. The store would obviously be closed for a few days.

By the time we left a few hours later, his body had been taken away and most of the emergency vehicles were gone. The car seemed far away with the street now clear and we walked to the car in a daze. My cousin had to stay behind and was in for a long night at the store.

We drove home without speaking, processing the event and crying as the reality set in that my uncle was no longer with us. The detective's last words kept replaying in my mind, "someone's life was saved by his quick actions," yet he was still gone. How is that fair? I couldn't get myself to use the word 'dead' yet, only the word 'gone'. I tried to imagine what went through his mind as he quickly assessed the situation and followed his instinct. Years of training for situations just like this and now he had used that training and paid with his life. I wondered if his emotions had played a role in his actions or if he could still remain objective while protecting his business.

We arrived home to two people sobbing at the table. Mom and dad pulled my brother and I together with them and we all embraced.

We stood together, sobbing, for a long time then dad asked me to go make some tea so he could share what we had learned about what had transpired. We stayed up chatting over tea not wanting to go to bed even though most of the questions that came up were left unanswered. We realized that we could run many 'what if?' scenarios but that it would not do us any good. We would have to wait for more answers as the investigation continued. Dad's primary question was when his body would be released so we could lay him to rest. I noticed that dad had emotionally distanced himself by saying 'the body' instead of using my uncle's name.

We each took turns getting some shuteye on the couch, though not really any deep sleep before we all got moving again.

The rays of the rising sun were reflecting on the kitchen floor when I awoke. Dad was on the phone. He finished his call and came over to hug me when he saw me get up.

"Would you get us something to eat? I'm going to freshen up then we'll get going. We have to go make funeral arrangements and I need to go see what's happening with the store. You and I can go help get it ready to open again in a few days. It's what he would want. Thank you son." He squeezed my shoulder as he left.

How does one deal with a senseless tragedy? This question had come up numerous times and remained unanswered. Perhaps there was a book on how to deal with this stupid, cruel act of violence. A book! Of course the library, I would find time to go see Andrew.

The toast popped out and I reached over mindlessly. Why? He was a good man. Why?

"What did I tell you about that? Oh yes, I remember exactly what I said – Love and Forgiveness. No matter what it is. Love and forgiveness plus prayer and affirmation will get you back on track and keep you there. Do you remember, do you?"

The voice seemed to reverberate in the kitchen as the question was repeated. I knew I wasn't dreaming because toast doesn't burn when you are asleep. It was my uncle, back to remind me of his lessons.

I sat down and verbally acknowledged that I had heard him.

"I hear you. Hopefully I'm not hallucinating from lack of sleep but yes, I heard you sir." I couldn't see him though I could clearly hear him.

I knew it was real as he continued. "No sir crap, it's me. Listen doc, you can cry for me and you can be sad but don't you dare let my death hold you back. Was it senseless? Sure! Violent? Yes! Unnecessary? Maybe? Everything happens for a reason, even if the reason is not obvious at the time. Listen, we all have choices in life and each choice has a consequence. I made my choice now you must go make yours. I've lived every day as if it were my last day on earth since way back in my police days. I embraced and appreciated every single one of them completely. Strive to learn something new every day from every person you meet. I'm gone physically so all you have are my memories and my lessons.

Learn from my life and from my death. You have a lot more to do in this world. Go find more mentors and keep learning. Keep improving yourself then become a mentor and share of yourself with others. When you do you'd better take that responsibility seriously doc. My impact on the world and on each individual life that I touched that is my legacy. My legacy will live on and that was always my intention. My life is over, yours is just beginning – Go live it, go make it a better world. Be better for you regardless of who attempts to hold you back. That is your legacy."

"Is that toast for me?" Dad had sat down at the table.

"What? Oh sorry yes, yes it is. I was just thinking about the last conversation I had with him yesterday. It's like he was right here chatting to me."

"When? Just a few minutes ago? Impossible. He was just upstairs chatting to me while I was getting dressed, "dad replied between bites. Then without missing a beat he continued,

"Maybe that's the upside, you can be in many places at once," he smiled a slight smile and I returned it. This would be an emotional day for all of us and he was injecting a bit of humor into the situation. I appreciated his attempt at lightening the load.

My uncle's house was crowded when we arrived. There was a constant stream of people stopping by to offer their condolences.

My aunt looked exhausted but was doing her best to keep going. Dad and I walked over to where she was sitting with her boys. She stood up and hugged us, then requested that we all go upstairs for a private conversation.

She relayed that she had called the coroner's office and was told that his body would be released the following morning. The police would be done at the main store in a few days then we would be allowed back on the premises.

We went over my uncle's wishes and what he would have wanted. He had always insisted that his funeral be a private family affair with a life celebration for everyone else. We discussed how to fulfill his wishes and made the arrangements for his funeral, his life celebration and when the stores would reopen. My cousin offered to make signs for his 'celebrate my life' event and post them at all three stores. She sent my cousins off to start making some calls but asked dad and I to stay.

"Thank you both for all that you are doing," she started, "I know how much he trusts and respects you and how much your family means to him." She spoke in the present tense as if he were in the other room. I understood why she was speaking that way and I nodded as she turned to speak to dad.

"I have a huge favor to ask and I'll understand if you say no to my request. We have a lot to do right now but the business must go on. You are the only one in the family that I can ask and I know he would approve. My question to you is whether you can take an extended leave from work to help us run the business while I get all his affairs in order. It sounds like little one has already decided not to go back to school so he can start training with his brother. Is there any way you could take some time off to help us?"

Then she turned to me. "I know you've been helping out at the main store while you are out of school. Do you mind continuing to do so for a little while longer? You cousin will continue to give you a ride once we get going again in a few days."

I waited for dad to answer first. He was a take-charge kind of man like his brother and his current managerial position made him the ideal person. The only question was whether he could *or would* be able to get off work.

"How long do you think you'll need me?" was his first question to her.

"I don't know. What do you think it would take to get it all done? Maybe it cannot be done and I should look into closing one or both of the other stores. What do you think?"

She seemed sincere with her comments although a small part of me wondered if this was part of a well-executed plan. She had an interesting choice of words; emotional words that would make dad feel like he had no choice in the matter.

His answer confirmed what I knew he'd say and her gratitude afterwards seemed real and sincere. Three simple words from dad and he had a new career path. "Consider it done."

I also said yes to working at the store, simply saying, "I'll do what I can," with a reminder that I made no guarantee about how long I would stay. I didn't tell her that I was doing schoolwork again and needed time to study.

Dad called his boss as soon as we got home to request the month of vacation time that he had accrued. Mom, my brother and I went out to buy a new shirt for the funeral. My brother had a tough time deciding what to buy. My choice was easy and required no thinking; I chose the exact light blue button down shirt that my uncle had worn on his last day.

The funeral was not as emotionally draining as I feared it would be. My uncle was buried with full military honors and thanked for service to his country even though he had not died in the line of duty. I left the cemetery sad yet proud of the man's many achievements. The family gathered for a light lunch at his house then left to prepare the hall where everyone had been invited for his 'celebrate my life' event.

I knew my uncle was a respected man in the community but the response was unbelievable. I stopped counting after 3000 and the people just kept coming. I was glad to see Dr. Ray among the many that showed. It was amazing to me how many had chosen to show their respect for the man given such short notice.

The stories that were shared about him kept us laughing and crying well into the night. It was a fantastic way to celebrate and honor the man who had touched so many lives.

It was his legacy and the effect was more far reaching than I could ever have imagined. In my mind he was a shining example of the man that Andrew was helping me become. I prayed that I could be a small percentage of the man that he was. It was a true celebration and we all felt his presence and spirit. It was a night I shall cherish forever. We were exhilarated and exhausted when we arrived home. Mom reminded me that I had a chiropractic appointment the next day and she would take off work to come get me.

I collapsed in bed recalling some of the silly stories about the man I knew and loved. I could see a lot of dad in him and I appreciated having dad in my life. I would honor my uncle by forgiving dad and work on having a better relationship with him. I had the power of choice and I chose to now make my dad part of my life. I had to continue the legacy that my uncle had left behind.

I slept in the next day and everyone was gone when I got up. Mom had left a note saying that she would pick me up at nine so she could get back to work. I was ready when she arrived and looked forward to seeing Dr. Ray again. It was different walking into his office upright this time instead of seeing it from a wheelchair.

"Welcome back. You may not remember me from the other night, I'm Claudia." The lady said as I walked in. She came out from behind her desk and extended her hand.

"Good to meet you Claudia," I replied as I shook her hand. She handed mom a chart to sign and turned back to me, "would you like a tour of the office now that you're not in pain?"

"Yes, I would. I would also like to know how the doctor did what he did the other night. It was a miracle."

She smiled, "not really a miracle. We see many amazing changes here in people of all ages. We are a family chiropractic office and we see everyone from newborns to the elderly. That's the play area over there and you can see the hundreds of photos of the children that we have helped over the years. This is the open adjusting area here. Dr. Ray, look who's back."

He came over to shake my hand. "Good to see you. Looks like you responded well to your adjustment. There's an open table over there, go ahead and lie on your stomach with your face on the paper and I'll be right with you.

Again, my condolences but boy, what a way to celebrate his life! I've already told my wife I want a party like that when I'm gone." He walked over to mom and repeated his statements while I went to lie down.

I was pleasantly surprised at how comfortable the table was. He finished with the person next to me then came over to me. "OK, let's see how you're doing today." His hands gently touched my neck first then he methodically moved down my spine. He would stop in certain places and I'd feel a gentle tug or push, before he moved on. He had only spent a few minutes with me when he announced that he was done. It didn't seem like he had done anything and I wasn't expecting much since I wasn't in pain like the first time.

I pushed up from the table into a standing position, took a few steps and "whoa!" escaped my lips again. I thought I was doing fine before this yet now I felt even better. I felt lighter on my feet, taller and loose all over. My breathing was deeper and I felt a warm sensation as the blood flowed down to my extremities. So this is what my uncle had been raving about. So this was chiropractic care.

"Does that feel good?" I heard him ask.
"Very much so, yes, thank you." I was about to describe all the changes I was feeling, but refrained, choosing instead to simply enjoy what felt like a new body to me.

Dr. Ray smiled as he observed me walk around the office and contort my body without any restrictions or pain.
"Here's the information I promised you," he started to say, "Never mind, you keep enjoying the changes in your body. I'll give it to your mom. Here you go ma'am." He handed mom an envelope. "Call me at any time to discuss any issues or problems you have with the forms."

"Great, thank you doc," mom replied smiling as she motioned for me to join her before we walked over to Claudia at the front desk, "how much do we owe you for today and for last time?"

"Let's see, "she opened the file and scanned the chart, "two visits and the initial exam, you total is ….Hmm! Hold on, I'll be right back," she said as she walked into the main room to find Dr. Ray.

Mom and I looked at each other as we waited for her return. All we wanted to do was pay our bill. What exactly did Claudia see in my chart that made her walk away from us?

Claudia returned with the open chart, "Yes, this is correct. Your total is zero. Your uncle took care of it the other night and prepaid for six visits. All we have to do is make another appointment for you. How about Friday?"

"Son of a gun. Are you serious? When did he do that?" mom asked after hearing the news.

"I don't know, but you are all paid up. What time on Friday works for you?" Claudia replied looking at the schedule.

"We'll have to call you," she looked at me, "We don't know what time you are working yet so we'll call to schedule."

"No problem, enjoy the rest of your day," Claudia replied and turned to help the next person in line.

Mom was crying when we left, "son of a gun. The man is gone and he's still taking care of everyone. Thank you." She said looking up to the sky. She dropped me at home and went back to work. I waved as I watched her leave then left the house as soon as she was out of sight.

I had to go speak to Andrew.

Chapter 21 ~ Vision

I found him washing windows inside the library. I had not seen him in a long time and I took a few minutes to observe him in action. He was completely focused on what he was doing and every move was deliberate and intentional. I watched as he deftly maneuvered his sponge and squeegee, cleaning the window without spilling a drop.

"You missed a spot," I said coming up behind him. "Kunjani? my brother. I haven't seen you in a while, have you been well?"

"Not really. I've been through quite a bit lately, including a death in the family. How about you, are you well?"

"I'm sorry to hear that. Yes, I have been very well. Thank you for asking. Tell me all about what has been happening. I won't even make you work for it. It is a slow day today and I'm caught up with all my work. In fact, I'm leaving early today."

"Oh. That's unusual, is everything Ok? I won't keep you if you are leaving."

"Yes, all is well. Walk with me while we chat. I only have two more windows to clean. Tell me what's been going on my brother."

I started from the last time I had seen him. Andrew would stop me and ask a few detailed questions or make a brief comment as I continued sharing.

"I know chiropractor, I have been and it feel good I know," he chimed in after my painful encounter. I told him about my declaration in Dr. Ray's office and how his spider/ant analogy had helped me with my decision to return to school. I told him about my uncle's visit and about working at the store.

I went into detail about the changes my uncle had noticed and the lessons he had taught me. Andrew humbly bowed his head when I reported that my uncle had given his approval for him to keep teaching and being a mentor to me. My voice changed as I ended with the details of the death and the magnitude of his legacy that emerged during his celebration of his life event.

"Why do you keep saying killed? Why do you not say he was murdered?" was his first comment after I had finished.

"I don't really know. I suppose it was murder wasn't it? Yes, he was murdered. I can say that word. Now that I've said it I realize that I cannot put him to rest until the bad guys are caught."

"What if they are never caught and it remains unsolved for years. Based on what you've said it will always be an issue. Your uncle was a wise man. You should apply what he has taught you. Forgive, my brother, forgive. You must forgive them with love so you can move on. Let them go, pray for them if you wish. Is it easy? No! Can you do it right now? No! At some point though you will have to forgive and move forward or you will be sucked back into the old you that you've been working on leaving behind. They will get what they deserve for their actions. Forgive doesn't mean forget, it means letting go of what is holding you back. Do you remember our first lesson about cleaning your mind and having the right mindset? This is a real life example of how to apply it. Remember, these lessons are no good if you keep them in your head or on the bookshelf. They will only work when you apply them in your life. I know, I know, you're going to tell me it's not easy. Well it's not supposed to easy my brother."

"No, it's not easy. I cannot stand the thought of these guys being out there and doing this to someone else. Maybe they'll make a mistake and get caught so justice can be done."

"That's not up to you or me. Why spend time . . . no waste time, wondering and looking back when you can use your energy to look forward. Maybe I can show you. How much time do you have today?"

I looked over at the clock on the wall. "I have to be home by four. Why do you ask?"

"Come with me." He said as he clocked out and led me downstairs. "Good bye," he said as he went up to each of clerks before we left the building.

He paused for moment and scanned the parking lot then waved to the driver of an old, rusty and loud vehicle pulled into the parking lot.

"Wait here," he said and went over to speak to the driver. He looked over in my direction and motioned for me to come over to the back of the car.

"Get in. This is Thembo." He introduced me to the driver who nodded silently. He was a big man who looked uncomfortable crammed in the driver's seat of this little car. I knew he was a tall man by how far his seat was pushed back. He turned out of the parking lot headed for the highway.

Andrew was in the front seat and turned to face me. I was sitting on an old blanket in the backseat. "If it's not too loud for you we can continue chatting. What do say?"

"I say we chat away and shout if we have to. Where are we going?" I answered and even the driver smiled. Good, I thought, now I knew that he understood English.

"You'll see soon enough. Let's just say I know it will help you move forward. Tell me my brother, when do you think you'll be back to work?"

"Probably the day after tomorrow. I don't know how I'm being scheduled yet since I need study time now as well. I may not get a chance to see you again with things being so, so different now." I was speaking in a normal voice and he had no trouble hearing me.

We were on the highway for a while and my expression must have changed when I read the road sign. Andrew had been looking at the driver and was speaking to him in Xhosa while listening to me.

"Are you afraid my brother?" he asked when he turned back to me, "I know you saw the sign."

"Yes, actually I am. I've never been to the township before. Is it safe for me there? You know I trust you but I'm still concerned."

"Is it safe for you'" he asked in Xhosa. "I hope so," he answered as Thembo smiled. He switched to English. "I'm just joking my brother, it will be safe for you.

It's the middle of the day and we will avoid going past any dangerous zones. We will not be there long anyway."

As we entered the township I looked around at the dusty unpaved roads and the thousands of shacks sitting together in rows. We drove slowly to avoid all the people who were in the narrow makeshift streets. We entered an open space and Andrew called back to me "Get down. Quick. Stay down. OK, come back up."

I looked back and saw that an army patrol had gone by but had not stopped. We went down a few more narrow streets and parked.

"Get out on that side and follow Thembo. Be quick, do not look around or speak to anyone, just follow him. Only leave with one of us once you are inside, no matter what. Stay low and stay alert. Now go."

Thembo came around the car to the side closest to the shack and opened the car door for me.

We moved quickly and entered crouching through a side door. We were crouched down in front of metal shelves with Thembo in the lead. The shelves were stocked with an array of canned goods. On our left we passed a lady with her back turned towards us leaning out over a small counter in front of an enlarged space where a window would typically be. She turned and nodded to Thembo while she reached for a few cans and handed them to someone outside. She accepted money and made change below her then leaned out again to make another sale. We were inside a grocery store of some kind. I glanced around the room as he kept moving and saw more products and merchandise on the many shelves lining the room.

 He led me through another door where the stench of raw meat filled the air. It had a similar setup, selling meat through a window.

The next door opened into a bigger room with a counter on one side. It was painted a burnt orange and smelled of cigarette smoke. There were three round tables in the room with six to eight chairs around them. Six men played dominoes at one of them. Two men looked right us, first at Thembo then at me as we entered. They nodded silently then turned their attention back to the game.

We stood up and walked across the room and out into the sunlight, passing three fire drums with meat grilling on it, toward a larger, fancier brick building on the other side of the open sand lot.

He stopped and knocked twice, waited, then knocked twice again. I heard the slide of two deadbolts and a key turn before the door opened. We entered a brightly painted room, a living room with a television on one side and a couch facing the door. Andrew was sitting on the couch.

"Welcome to my home, my brother. Welcome to my home. Come in, sit down," he said then turned to Thembo

"Thank you Thembo. Give me about thirty minutes then we must take him back. It should be an easy ride at that time yes? Get something to eat while I chat then come back. No drinking OK? That meat on the grill looks good, go get a sandwich."

"Yes, no problem. A sandwich sounds good. Enkosi (thank you)" Thembo replied then turned and headed back toward what I now realized was a restaurant where the men had been sitting.

"Would you like a drink? I know you have many questions but let's start with a drink. Do you drink tea?" Andrew turned to speak to the lady who had walked into the room, "Rooibos tea for me please and whatever he's having."

"Yes, tea would be great, thank you." I replied to both of them. After she had left I turned back to Andrew.

"This is your home? Looks like a great place you have here, much fancier than I would have imagined though. Why did you bring me here and why did we have to go through the other building first?"

Andrew smiled. "I wanted to make sure that you were not spotted AND I wanted you to see the businesses. My businesses. The first place is obviously the general store then you saw the butcher shop and the restaurant. I own them plus two more just like that around the township. They are doing very well and we are staying busy because my people do not want to risk leaving the township and getting arrested and charged with political activity right now."

My jaw dropped, "Are you serious, you are a businessman? I don't mean to judge but that is quite a surprise. Why are you working in a library so far away when you can be here running your business, I mean businesses."

The tea arrived. He personally served me before taking his tea and sitting across from me in the comfy chair in the corner. He took a few sips, savoring the taste of the warm beverage before he answered.

"I want to show you the big picture, my brother. You have been through a lot recently and you are stuck like I once was. My story may help you. You see when I was your age I had already been in and out of jail a few times. It started with stealing because we didn't have enough to eat. I told myself it was not stealing if I only took what I needed to feed my family. My first arrest was for theft. It made me angry because I felt like I was doing what I had to do so we wouldn't starve. I was angry at the system and frustrated so I vowed to get rich. Then I got involved in gangs and they introduced me to drugs. I became a drug dealer making a lot of money at a young age. I was on top of the world. I even carried a gun because I was 'the man.' I was living the dream life on the outside yet dying on the inside. I had money yet I was still unhappy. The young guys in the township feared me and admired me as they watched me buy anything I wanted. I was showing the white man that I could survive in his world and not just be a stupid black man. Apartheid made me drop out of school and not get an education so I got street smart instead. I also got greedy in the process. My turning point in life, just like yours right now I'm sure, came quickly and unexpectedly."

He paused and sipped his tea. He lowered his voice and I could hear the emotion as he spoke. I waited patiently. He coughed, took a breath and continued.

"I was the man on the street, the go-to man when you needed your fix. I got word about a big drug deal and I was the only dealer big enough who could fill the order. What should have been the sale of a lifetime turned out to be the turning point that changed and as I later realized also saved my life.

It was an undercover operation and most of the guys who went with me were either killed or arrested, probably still sitting in jail. I got away but was madder than before. The white man had set me up. I blamed everyone except myself and vowed to get even.

I had money and I had power in my township but I didn't know what to do to get around being black in a white man's world.

I was in town one day when I accidently found myself in the middle of a political rally. I saw blacks and coloureds, even some whites protesting and it surprised me. A white guy came up to me and asked me for money to support the party.

Can you believe it?

A white man came to ask a black man for money. I was wearing an expensive suit so that may have been part of it too. I was hooked and started learning more about politics. It was this same white man, Simon who started teaching me what I've been teaching you. He made me realize that I was killing my own people with drugs and that getting involved in the struggle for equality was a much better way to spend my time and my money.

He taught me many things and you are now ready for this lesson too. After Mindset and Intention comes Vision.

Vision, he explained by asking me what I wanted to contribute to the world. Did I want to be known for killing people or for helping them?

I was killing my own people with drugs, yet with the right Vision I could help them instead. He helped me realize what my vision was and you have seen the results with the businesses I now own.

Vision my brother, is the ability to see something before it even exists. It has to be so powerful that nothing, including your current circumstances will get in the way. Share your vision with those around you to make it more real. Many people confuse vision with dreams but they are complete opposites. When you wake up from a dream it is gone while your vision keeps you awake. Your vision must be behind everything you do and directs you to set goals along the way and take the positive action steps toward every goal no matter what comes you way. "

"What is your vision, my brother? I know what it is because you have told me many times but you have forgotten because you are too distracted right now.

Vision doesn't care about obstacles. When your vision is strong enough anything, or any one that gets in your way simply delays you slightly, that is all. The future is not written. The past is behind you. Stop living in the past and blaming, look forward to move forward. Notice I didn't say look ahead, I said look forward.

When you look ahead with a negative mindset all you will see are obstacles and problems. Your mindset, your intention and your vision can and should change as you grow in life. What seemed like the right decision at the time may not be right for you now. That's fine. You get to choose your path regardless of what anyone else thinks. It is your life my brother. You choose where you want to go and what you want to do. You must move toward your vision for yourself, no one else matters. You, my brother, have a whole new chapter ahead of you and you are the author of your future. Enjoy every moment. Create an amazing life for yourself starting right now. Do you really want to spend your life unhappy behind the counter working for your cousin? Is this what you want, what your parents want or what your uncle would have wanted for you? What is your vision my brother, what is your vision?"

"Thank you for sharing your story with me but that is your life not mine. You know that money is an issue at home and at least I'm helping out now by working as well. I've already committed to going back to school. Isn't that enough?" I felt like I had to justify my behavior to him even though I knew that Andrew was right. I had complained to him many times about how miserable I was at the store and what I thought of my cousin's business skills.

"You tell me, is it? Tell me my brother," he asked again, "Is being at the store part of your vision? Remind me again what your favorite part of the week is?"

I should have known that he would use my own words against me to make his point.

"Are you really going to make me say it? Damn, you are so irritating when you are right. Yes, my favorite part is going to Dr. Ray and learning more about what he does and how amazing the human body is. My dream is to do what he does someday. I know I said dream because that's what it is, it's only a dream."

"It's time to go." Thembo had come back into the room. The car is right here. Andrew, do you want to go too or should I just take him back myself?"

"No, you take him. Sweep your mind my brother and let me know what you hear when there is nothing in the way. You have the steps and you have the knowledge now the action steps are up to you.

Andrew turned to Thembo, "Thank you and be careful." Then he looked at me, "The answer to your question earlier about why I'm working at the library. I am the author of my future and I do what I *want* to do every day not what I *have* to do. There is a big difference between the two. My businesses are doing well and making money but, as I've explained to you, I've had money before. Someday you will know as I now do that money by itself does not bring you happiness. It's good to have it but it should not be the reason you get up every day. I work where I do to continue making a difference in people's lives outside of my world, my reality. Besides, I learn by listening and observing then I apply those lessons to my business here as it grows and expands. Go well my brother go well. I'm sure I'll speak to you again soon. Remember that you are the author of your future."

The drive back to the library seemed to go quickly as I contemplated what Andrew had told me and showed me.

Thembo dropped me off at the library and I ran home quickly with Andrew's words still ringing in my head. I would never have imagined that he was a successful business owner. That was the point, wasn't it? I had judged him and he showed me how dangerous my mindset was before he took me on the amazing journey that brought me to where I currently was in my life. I could no longer settle for the mediocre, settle for what life had given me.

I wasn't happy, I knew it and he knew it. Heck even my cousin knew it yet I thought there was nothing I could do. That was the problem, I was thinking and it made me helpless. I had to shift my mindset again like I had previously done when I stood for something and joined the boycott. It was the right decision at the time and now I was changing my mind and going back to school.

My passion was not to spend the rest of my life in a grocery store. I have a choice and I choose to create my own path, my Vision. All the lessons I had learned from those around me; the lessons that life had taught me had led me to this moment in time.

I walked to the center of the living room in a daze and kneeled down. I put my hands together, looked out of the window to the sky and made a commitment to myself.

"Dear God, dear universe, dear loved ones. Thank you for bringing me to this point in my life. As of right now, at this very moment in time - I choose happiness. I choose the path to happiness regardless of current circumstances or obstacles. I choose this path so I can look back someday and say that it was my choice. I choose this path for myself, regardless of what others think or say. It is my choice. Whether I succeed or fail, whether I live or die, whether I make it or not, I choose my own destiny and my path to happiness. I choose, no matter what it takes, to finish school, go to college and follow my vision. The last lesson from my uncle was about leaving a lasting legacy and I refuse to let mine be as the guy behind the counter."

Vision: The power and ability to see what does not yet exist.

My mindset, intention and vision had guided my words and I was moving forward, onward and upward. I was sobbing on the living room floor and I let the tears run freely. Many images were flashing in my mind and I watched them pass by without thought or judgment. It was liberating to let my raw emotions release uninhibited. I was lightheaded when I arose and walked, almost floated out of the room to go freshen up.

I heard the garage door open and my name being called a few minutes later. My brother was home from school and both mom and dad were home.

Mom called my name again and when she saw me asked me to join all three of them at the table for a family meeting.

Mom spoke first. "I trust you had a good day boys? Did you have a good day at school?" She asked my brother then turned to me, "What have you been doing today? You look so much better after your visit this morning?" She waited while we both answered with a "fine" from my brother and a "yes, much better" from me. I offered no more due to my curiosity about the reason for this meeting.

"Your father and I want to speak about the new arrangements and the changes we all have to make for it to work."

Dad spoke next. "I'll be taking you to work from now on and you'll be spending time at whatever store needs you the most.

I'll be doing pick up and delivery between stores and you'll be seeing me a few times a day wherever you are working to get you what you need. Don't worry about having to work with your cousin all day; I'll take you between stores when needed or when you ask. Apparently your cousins already knew that you were going back to school and were told to do whatever they could to help you study or give you time off for study groups."

Dad was still speaking but I wasn't paying attention as I reflected on my uncle's words on that fateful morning. Now I understood what he meant by "I've made some arrangements with the boys," when he picked me up. I knew mom had called and told him about me going back to school and he wasted no time in doing what he could to support my decision. I wondered what his boys thought about their dad making 'special arrangements' for the cousin that they didn't like in the first place. I mentally thanked him and focused on dad again who was still speaking.

"Repairs have started at the store and all three will be open and running again in two days." I heard him say. I was amazed at how caring and loving he sounded. He DID care and he was a loving man. I could feel it now and I could hear it in his voice. The numbness and emptiness I was feeling after my uncle's murder was starting to dissipate as I felt the love of my family. I had questioned GOD, my vision and my reason for living and now it was becoming clearer, I was destined for college. As a family we seemed to be much closer and I was personally appreciating the sanctity of life.

"We are explaining this to you because you have to focus on your job so you can have longer lunches or shorter days at the store. Focus on your work when you are at the store and focus on your schoolwork during lunchtime and at night. You and I will go in tomorrow to help get everything ready." Dad and mom finished giving us more details then hugged us tightly.

"Let's go cook," mom said to my brother before turning to me. "Here you go," she said and handed me three more folders, "the rest of what you need to get caught up. You go study while we go cook." I took the folders, anxious to get going and knowing that I had made a commitment to move towards my vision. I stayed up late, eating in my room with my head in the books.

Chapter 22 ~ Goals & Action Steps

As expected, it felt different being at work again a few days later knowing that my uncle wasn't there but I quickly adapted to the new routine. Throughout the day there were reminders about him that I would quietly acknowledge then continue working without letting it distract me.

I ignored the snickering and snide remarks from my cousin who would often find me lying across a stack of boxes lounging three feet in the air for some quiet, private reading time between bites at lunchtime. I silently wondered if he realized the significance of me eating tuna sandwiches a few times a week. Knowing that I had my dad and my uncle's support felt great and made me work faster and more efficiently so I would have extra time during my lunch breaks to read and study. I did what had to be done to study, make it to the study groups and get ready for midterms while not ignoring my work duties.

To my surprise and delight I watched my cousins' attitudes change and soften over time. They would spend more time on the floor and respectfully speak to the employees. They cried and laughed along with us as customers, friends and employees shared stories about their dad.

Dad seemed to take on the role of the 'old wise man' as my cousins turned to him for information and advice about the business. I enjoyed the irony of seeing my dad become to my cousins what their dad had been for me. I started seeing how much he was like his brother and my view of him was dramatically changing. My respect for dad was cemented after a conversation with my cousin while we were sitting in the office. He had invited me to have lunch in his office and to take a break from the books.

We were chatting about how my studies were progressing when dad walked in. My cousin excused himself as he turned to speak to dad.

"May I please have a word with you sir?" he asked dad.

"Of course, what can I do for you? Do you mind if I eat while we chat?" Dad was warming the leftovers he had brought from his favorite meal last night.

"I was speaking to mom last night and we thought you should have this."

He walked over to the safe.

I heard the beeps as he entered the combination code and the soft clunk as he turned the handle and opened the door.

Dad had sat down at the desk across from me as my cousin returned and sat to my left between dad and me. He put two items on the desk in front of dad's plate as he spoke.

"This was one of dad's favorites," he continued as he removed the gun from the holster. "This is a 9 mm semi-automatic with 17 in the magazine and 1 in the chamber. It is easy to handle and has a safety right here."

Dad continued eating in silence, his face expressionless as my cousin continued with his show-and-tell presentation.

"It doesn't weigh very much and has a good sensitive trigger. I'll take you to the range after you take the class. Here is your application, I just need your signature here and I'll send it in. It shouldn't take very long because mom has already made some calls so they know your application's coming. Here's the info for the class at the shooting range." He handed dad the papers and the gun. Dad tapped the desk where he had pushed his plate aside without touching the weapon, motioning for him put them on the desk instead.

"Thank you for your description and for taking the time to get an application. I appreciate your and your mom's concern and I know that you mean well. I have much love and respect for your family and for your father as he had for me." Not just me, us," he said pointing to me then to himself. In conversation he would often tell me how he would and I quote 'take a bullet' for any of us.

He visited us often and I had many meaningful, in depth conversations with him on a variety of topics over the years.

We shared the same ideas and philosophies on many things, except one. This!" he pointed to the gun and the paper on the desk.

"I truly do appreciate what you are doing but I will not, in fact will never, carry, handle or even touch one of those. You are an adult and you do what you wish although I must admit that I am concerned. I see that both you and your brother have been carrying your weapons much more lately and although I understand why, it still concerns me. It's not my business so I haven't said anything to you. Again, thank you but definitely no thank you, not now not ever."

He turned to me as he arose to leave, "would you wash my dishes please?" He turned and left the office without saying anything else.

My cousin and I looked at each other after he left. I shrugged my shoulders, picked up the dishes and wrappers and left him sitting alone and bewildered in his office.

My dad shared my philosophy about guns. I didn't know that I thought to myself. Well, how would I know that? We didn't have a relationship until…well…until now.

My days starting blending together as I went from work to study groups to reading late into the night with eating and sleeping squeezed into the schedule somehow. I made it a point though to keep all my appointments with Dr. Ray and to make quick visits to Andrew to keep him updated, even if we were just passing by the library. There was no time for lessons only a quick greeting and update that he said he greatly appreciated. Even mom and dad hardly had time to chat to me and let me take naps in the car as they took turns driving me around.

I was nervous as exam time approached. The more we went over mock tests the more confident I felt about taking midterms. My efforts were paying off and I kept going. I could always catch up on sleep became my standard answer whenever someone mentioned how exhausted I looked.

The phone call came while I was at work and mom ran out to tell us when dad and I pulled into the driveway.

Mr. Petersen had personally called instead of letting us get the news in the mail. He could do it because the results for midterms came to him first.

This would not happen after the finals because it would be government administered. I had passed all my subjects. My grades were not great but they were passing grades. I could now confidently continue to prepare for finals.

Mom had prepared my favorite meal and we enjoyed a celebratory meal. I made sure to include my brother in the celebration who, we later learned when his report card arrived, had achieved his usual A's in all his subjects.

The possibility of actually graduating now and heading to college became a reality and my mindset became even stronger. Everything I did had purpose and I started sharing my vision of going to college with others.

I could never have imagined the response.
People started saying they would pray for me. I started praying more myself, asking for guidance to fulfill my purpose in life. Prayers often increase when we are desperate and need help instead of being used consistently in good time and bad. Even friends and family who were not religious would encourage me and mention that they would say a prayer for me. I discovered that they were referring to positive thoughts and affirmations. My cousin's former snickers and mocking magically turned into support as he started telling customers that I was finishing school so I could go to college. I started acting, feeling and speaking like I really could be a college student after my successful midterm results and it felt good. Nothing could get in my way. I found myself proudly announcing that I was going to be a doctor and saying I was going to leave the store.

My visits to Dr. Ray took on a new meaning for me as I paid more attention to what he did. His attitude to me had changed as well and he freely shared advice and patiently answered all my questions no matter how busy he was during my visits. He encouraged me and started calling me doc junior, even telling his patients about my plans.

It worked. The constant attention I was receiving from everyone fueled my passion and my Intention to be successful in my endeavors.

In fact, I took pride in boldly stating my vision whenever I could and never tired of hearing the varied responses. I was scared but my vision was stronger than my fear.

When you create your vision it becomes part of your mindset and there is no denying it. It eats away at you until your excuses and barriers become so annoying that you need to address them. I was working on my college plan. The plan made sense in my head except for two things that I still imagined would derail me.

I had found two potential obstacles that had to be addressed. I knew I could not move forward until I spoke to mom and dad and started planning my defense strategy for any excuses they would make. My dream was now my vision; I would be the doctor that my uncle had always seen in me.

The first issue was that even if I could get into college, where would I get the money for tuition? My parents had done a great job of hiding the fact that we were poor when I was younger yet there was no denying now that money for college was not available. All the money that I was earning went to mom, with me getting a set allowance from her every week. Growing up we always seemed to have what we needed, when we needed it. Dad's famous words were "God will provide it for us" and, I must admit, it seemed that God always did.

The second issue was that the course was not available in South Africa and I would have to go to America to study.

I asked mom and dad when we could have a meeting to address some concerns I had. I refused to tell them what it was until we could sit down together. Even though my packed schedule made it tough to set a time to I was determined to make it happen. We all finally agreed to chat after my final exams that were now quickly approaching. Dad had taken an indefinite leave of absence from his job and was focusing all his time on running the stores. He was working harder than my uncle ever had but he never complained. Mom had confided to me during one of our rides together that he would probably leave his job and continue what he was doing but couldn't get himself to make it official yet. His resignation letter was already written and ready to be mailed.

Mom and dad were very supportive, in fact acting somewhat strangely but I didn't have time to give it much thought.

One of their strange behaviors was the similarity of what they said to me.

Mom would give me 'you'll get it' and 'don't worry about anything' pep talks. "Focus on passing your exams. Whatever's on your mind that we need to chat about, we'll worry about later. We'll work it out O.K.?"

Dad also started giving me pep talks when we were together. "Focus on your finals, nothing else matters. Take off whenever you need and schedule whatever you have to. Nothing can and should stop you from moving forward. Let me know what you need. Your mom and I will do what we can, God will provide."

I felt their sincerity and I believed them. I kept setting the goals that would move me toward my vision and took the action steps to keep me going.

My room was scattered with stacks of papers ranging from goals and obstacles to school work and mock tests. I was glad that mom had not insisted I clean my room and even let me get away with not making my bed most of the time. Thankfully she also kept track of where I had to be and when I needed to be there. She modified her schedule to help me whether I was at the store or I had taken the day off to study for a mock test at the study group.

I was experiencing exhaustion, frustration, nervousness and excitement yet fortunately no pain or discomfort thanks to mom's diligence on keeping my appointments with Dr. Ray.

The weather had warmed and summer was almost here but my calendar was solely based on schoolwork and tests. I only knew it was late November because finals were a few days away.

Chapter 23 ~ Finals

A strange calm came over me as I sat down to take the first of six exams. I had taken the last few days off work to focus on studying, attending the study groups and taking the mock exams. I made sure to eat well last night and I was in bed by nine to get a good night's rest. My tummy was full from my favorite omelet breakfast and mom had dropped me off early at the test site. The security screening to get in to the building was time consuming yet did not bother me. I had been praying all morning and it had grounded and calmed my mind and my body for this pivotal moment. Even the expressionless, monotone instructions from the moderator amused me rather than make me nervous in the strict, professional atmosphere they were striving to create.

I waited for the moderator's permission to begin and opened the test booklet. I paid no attention to those around me and started the test. I followed the protocol that had been drilled into our heads by the teachers for the last few months. They had given us specific test-taking steps: start at the beginning of the test, answer all the questions that you can and skip the ones that you can't. When you get to the end come back and work on the tough questions until you have an answer. If you are unsure, go with your best guess and move to the next unanswered question. Trust your instinct since your first answer is most likely the correct one. When you have answered all the questions, review you answers once with your pencil on the desk and only change an answer if you know without a doubt that it is wrong. When you are done, close the test and rest your head on the desk until it's time to turn in your test.

I followed the same steps for all the tests, knowing that I had done my best to move toward my vision. My intention was to simply pass through this gate so I could move on to college.

I quickly got into the car without discussing the tests with any students or with mom who had come to pick me up after the long mentally exhausting day. Even though I was getting along well with dad now, I felt that mom would be more understanding if I asked to drive home in silence. She knew I was going straight to bed when we got home and she had agreed that it was a good plan. My cousin and dad had also insisted that I stay home the next day to rest before coming back to work. It felt good to finally lie down and completely relax both physically and mentally. The results would arrive by mail in ten to twelve days. It was noon the next day before I finally stirred and came out of my room. I took an extra long, hot shower and took my time getting dressed. I took a cup of coffee outside to enjoy the sunny day and again mentally release all the tension.

I didn't care whether I passed or failed; my results were unimportant to me. The only part that mattered was that my finals were over. As I arose to go back inside the house, the reflection caught my eye. There was a large, beautiful spider web above the outside light by the front door.

Chapter 24 ~ Mindset Determines Outcome

The dreaded meeting took place after work on Sunday after we had supper. I insisted that my brother stay for the meeting as well. They listened intently as I explained my concerns about going off to college and someday making a difference in the world and changing people's lives. Surprisingly no one interrupted me and they waited till I was done speaking before replying.

Mom spoke first. "Yes, we know that you'll have to go to America to study. What you don't know is that arrangements are already being made and all we are waiting for are your results. You said this is what you wanted so Dr. Ray has been helping me get everything ready for you to go. He has already written a letter of recommendation for you and has committed and insisted on paying for half your airfare. He has already spoken to the American consulate about what you need for your visa and to the school that he's recommending for you."

My body language must have changed because she smiled proudly about her covert planning. I was about to reply but dad spoke before I could answer.

"We are all proud of what you've done and who you've become. I've watched you stay focused and sacrifice a lot to get everything done. I have no doubt that you will get the results that you want now and as you continue moving forward. Apparently your uncle was proud of you too. I've been holding onto this for a while now and couldn't tell you about it because I knew it would make you lose focus.

When they went through your uncle's closet they found this," he handed me a thick envelope. It was stuffed with cash and I started crying when I turned it over. The front of the envelope read: DOC COLLEGE FUND.

I read the date on the upper right corner; it was dated the day of my announcement in Dr. Ray's office.

We were all crying and hugging and crying. I was deeply honored, speechless and overwhelmed with everything that we had shared. I felt humbled and I felt loved. I excused myself and went to my bedroom. First to say a prayer of gratitude then to rest so it could all sink in. Now all I needed were my final results. I could confidently state that I had done my best yet I included a prayer that my results would not be the obstacle that stopped me from reaching my vision. I started counting down the days, excited yet dreading the outcome. The day finally came. I watched through the bedroom window as he did what he did so well. His smiling face irritated me today as he waved to the neighbors and pulled up to our house.

Today was different because he held my future in his hands. His deliveries had helped me learn about customs and cultures from around the world as my pen friends shared their lives, their joys and their sorrows with me by mail. The mailman was my best friend around the holidays and especially around my birthday when I anxiously waited to see who had sent me birthday cards and more importantly the birthday cash that came in many of them. Today was not one of those days. I had secretly hoped that he would somehow have forgotten our mail and I would be spared another day but I knew that I was just putting off the inevitable. I opened the front door and waved to him as he pulled away. I took a deep breath as I walked to the mailbox. It wasn't far from the front door to the road where the old wooden mailbox sat on its post as it had for the past sixteen years and I took my time to traverse that short distance.

I felt like a prisoner walking to his execution. I pulled out the stack he had left and started flipping through slowly, scanning the envelopes until I saw it. The envelope with the official 'Department of Education' stamp on the upper left hand corner was about half way down and I stopped when I saw it. I briefly thought about putting the mail back in the mailbox but that thought quickly passed.

My report card had arrived. I was home alone and I hesitated on whether or rip it open or wait until tonight when everyone was home. I ripped it open.

'Congratulations you have passed your final exams.'

I scanned the page:

English:	C
Mathematics:	C
Afrikaans:	C
Physics:	C
Xhosa:	B
Biology:	C

I realized that I had been holding my breath and started coughing. I looked at the page again after my coughing spell to make sure that I had read it correctly. The words had not changed. I ran into the house and let out a loud scream then starting jumping around the kitchen. Yes! Yes! Yes! I was a high school graduate! I really was a high school graduate.
dropped to my knees. I stayed down for a while letting all the emotions bubble up and release. I went through many emotions from feeling humble and grateful to proud and excited. It had taken the combined efforts of many and now the results were here.

Mom had already called this morning asking if the mail had arrived yet. She sighed with disappointment when I said no and gave me an "O.K., I'll call back later. Don't worry, you'll get it. We'll deal with it when it comes," pep talk before she hung up.

There would be much to do between working at the store to save money to making travel plans and sending in all the paperwork for college. I had declined applying for a passport when my parents asked me to do so months ago. I wanted to wait until I knew for sure that I was going before I held a passport to the world. I had to go tell one other person first before I called mom and dad with the news.

I enjoyed the summer weather as I walked to the library with my head held high and my results in my pocket. I had to go tell my friend and mentor right away so I could be home when mom called again.

Proceeding up the path to the front door of the library, I saw him pruning the bushes along the walkway in the sun. He was a tall man with big hands holding the pruning shears. I couldn't help but smile as I heard him whistling while he cheerfully gyrated in a mock dance with the bush he was trimming. He moved gracefully even with his work boots on. I was surprised to see him wearing an American style baseball cap and blue jeans instead of overalls, as I would have expected.

"Kunjani? (How are you?) Andrew" I screamed excitedly as I approached him. "I have news for you."

"My brother, good to see you. From your mood I can guess what the news is. Tell me, my brother tell me."

"This is where it all started sir, do you remember? It seems much longer than the eight or nine months since you first messed with my mind. Now I owe you so much and I'll be forever grateful to you for how far you've helped me come. My results arrived today, just a few minutes ago actually and I had to come let you know right away. I am a high school graduate. Can you believe it? I am a high school graduate. I did it! I did it! I did it with your help and guidance. Thank you my friend. Enkosi Kakhulu! Yeehaa! Woohoo!"

Andrew smiled and put the shears down. He gave me a big hug and a few pats on the back.

"Eish! My brother. Eish! Congratulations to you. You've worked hard and now you've seen the results." He smiled broadly and hugged me again. "Yes, I remember that first day very well. You had much to sweep and clear your mind for good things to enter and now here you are, a confident young man with plans for college. You have learned much and you now know the steps to take to move ahead. You've learned how Mindset comes first, then Intention, Vision, Goals and Action steps. There is one more piece you must know. You must start with Love. Love yourself, love what you do and love where you are. You must love yourself enough to know when you need help and ask for help before you reach a point of desperation. No matter how good you are doing you can always accept help when given with love." He paused to make sure I was listening.

"You must love what you do so you can accept failure. Your outcome will not always be what you desire but that doesn't mean that you should give up. Mindset is like rewiring your brain and when something isn't working, change the action step and keep moving. Ask for help and guidance and even pay someone to help you so you can shorten the road to your vision. Do you understand my brother?"

"Yes sir, I understand." I answered confidently. I was no longer the scared boy he had met just a short time ago.

"I'll say it again, I cannot thank you enough. I'll be back often to keep you updated. From what Dr. Ray has said it will take a few months to get everything arranged."

He nodded. "Good. You may now officially start getting excited Mr. College man."

My face changed as I smiled broadly. "I like the sound of that, say it again."

"Mr. College man. By the way, I never answered a question that you asked me. The question about why I showed you my home and my businesses."

"Yes, you're right. You avoided it at the time."

"The answer my brother was to show you that you could achieve whatever you wish to achieve in life. Remember that your past is your past. It is part of who you are yet does not, I repeat does not, define who you are you. You are lucky in that you are starting without the baggage that I've had. You are leaving the country but the country will never leave you. Strive for want you wish to achieve and make your efforts consistent, incremental and most importantly ethical. As you help others they will help you and you'll be surprised at who will step forward when there is no judgment. Remember where you've come from my brother. Change yourself first before you change the world."

"I will. Thank you my brother, thank you."

"Go celebrate my brother, you've earned it. Thank you for letting me know right away. Now get out of here. You have much to do."

I whistled as I floated home to call mom and dad to give them the great news.

"Start the ball rolling, let the preparations begin," I said out loud. I knew what the outcome would be. I was going to college.

ABOUT THE AUTHOR

Known as 'The Mindset Coach', Zaahir 'Dr. Z.' Hendricks grew up during the Apartheid era in South Africa. He achieved his vision of attaining his chiropractic degree and built a busy family chiropractic office in the suburbs of Chicago, Illinois. Now he coaches worldwide online and shares his message as an inspirational speaker, health and wellness coach and change agent around the world. His engaging, informative presentations on Mindset, Health and related topics have been well received by corporations, associations and learning institutions as well as thousands of individuals through his conferences and home study courses. He lives with his amazingly patient and supportive spouse and is still proudly South African.

The MDO coaching series is available online at:
http://www.mindsetdeterminesoutcome.com

Join and share in our facebook group:
https://www.facebook.com/groups/yourmindset/

www.ingramcontent.com/pod-product-compliance
Lightning Source LLC
Chambersburg PA
CBHW031259090426
42742CB00007B/525